Elimination & Endplays

JAMES MARSH STERNBERG MD (DR J)

AND

DANNY KLEINMAN

authorHOUSE

AuthorHouse™
1663 Liberty Drive
Bloomington, IN 47403
www.authorhouse.com
Phone: 833-262-8899

Published by AuthorHouse 02/17/2022

ISBN: 978-1-6655-5227-1 (sc)
ISBN: 978-1-6655-5226-4 (e)

Also by James Marsh Sternberg

Playing to Trick One; No Mulligans in Bridge
Trump Suit Headaches; Rx for Declarers
The Finesse; Only a Last Resort
Blocking and Unblocking
Shortness – A Key to Better Bidding
Michaels Meets the Unusual
From Zero to Three Hundred; A Bridge Journey

James Sternberg With Danny Kleinman

Second Hand High; Third Hand Not So High
An Entry, An Entry; My Kingdom For an Entry
L – O – L   Loser on Loser
Elimination and Endplay
In Search of a Second Suit

CONTENTS

Chapter 2. Trump Endplays

DEDICATION

To:
JOEL FEISS, MD

My close friend, a terrific doctor who has kept me going, and a fine author, who inspired me to become a writer myself.

Thanks for everything

ACKNOWLEDGEMENTS

This book would not have been possible without the help of several friends. Frank Stewart, Michael Lawrence, Anne Lund, Eddie Kantar and Marty Bergen, all provided suggestions for material for the book.

I am forever indebted to Hall of Famer Fred Hamilton and the late Bernie Chazen, without whose guidance and teaching I could not have achieved whatever success I have had in bridge.

And of course I want to thank Vickie Lee Bader, whose love and patience helped guide me thru the many hours of this endeavor.

James Marsh Sternberg MD
Palm Beach Gardens FL
mmay001@aol.com

INTRODUCTION

Card play at bridge embraces both declarer play and defense. Hundreds of books have been written about it. Our approach here, as in our previous books, is to focus on a particular deal type. Repeated experience with a theme makes it easier to recognize deal types and employ the appropriate techniques for each.

In this as in our previous books, we show deals as they were misplayed at rubber bridge or its sister form of contest, team play at IMPs, Take each misplayed deal as a challenge to find a better line—usually one that works, but no guarantees. An 80% play fails 20% of the time, but is significantly better than a 60% play and much better than a 40% play.

Usually you will see a deal in which declarer falls short of his contract by one trick. Do not concern yourself with overtricks. In the forms of contest assumed here, making and breaking contracts is the objective.

A finesse is the most obvious and simplest technique for getting the one additional trick needed to make an iffy contract. But we encourage you to look at alternatives. Here the alternative to an ordinary finesse is a finesse that you can get an opponent to take for you, sometimes called a "free" finesse. The cost lies only in the preparation: strip an opponent of safe exit cards before putting him in to lead.

A common and important line of play is elimination play, eliminating the side suits to removes an opponent's safe exit cards before throwing him in to make a fatal lead.

More than most other deal types, endplays require planning and preparation. We have supplied complete layouts at the top of each page for ease of reference, but you will benefit more from the book if you look only at your own hand and the dummy, covering the other two hands while working out the best plays, and looking at the entire deal afterwards for confirmation.

What Is An Endplay?

An endplay consists of giving an opponent a trick when he has no safe exit card. It is also called a "Strip and throw-in," as the first step is removing the opponent's exit cards. An opponent is put on lead at a strategic moment when his play will cost him one or more tricks. Most commonly this constitutes giving declarer a free finesse or a ruff-sluff. Sometimes declarer may be forcing defender to break a suit that declarer could not break without costing himself a trick. Sometimes too, declarer may lack an entry to dummy or his hand and may be forcing the defender into leading next to that hand.

How can you recognize and execute an endplay? There are four basic steps.

Recognize a suit that you need a defender to play (sometimes called the tuxedo).
Identify the exit card you will feed to the defender to throw him in (the feeder).
Eliminate the defender's safe exit cards (the strip).
Play the throw-in exit card to put defender on lead.

What are the indicators that an endplay may be possible? The first is the presence of long trumps in both hands. This means when a defender is forced to win a trick, a subsequent ruff-sluff possibility exists. Another is a fragile suit holding, for example ◊J43 opposite ◊Q76. Assuming the two top honors are split between the defenders, whoever plays this suit first loses a trick.

Other combinations where you would prefer not to go first include:

KJ4	K6(5)	A3
	opposite	
A103	43(2)	Q4

In a variation, ◊A104 opposite ◊K95, an endplay offers a 50% chance for a third trick (split honors) instead of almost no chance at all.

Suits that can be neither discarded nor developed for tricks with intermediates or long cards are called "sterile suits." Some examples would include:

54	A4	K65
	opposite	
87	63	A32

You can cash all your winners and use the low card as the feeder or exit card for the throw-in.

Is there a basic technique to follow? Yes, and it's quite simple. If this seems too basic for you, bear with me. I'm sure the hands to follow will pique your interest.

Let's look at an entire deal to see how this works.

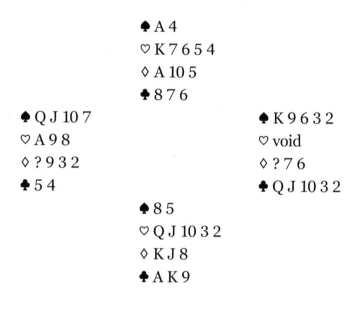

♠ A 4
♡ K 7 6 5 4
◊ A 10 5
♣ 8 7 6

♠ Q J 10 7   ♠ K 9 6 3 2
♡ A 9 8   ♡ void
◊ ? 9 3 2   ◊ ? 7 6
♣ 5 4   ♣ Q J 10 3 2

♠ 8 5
♡ Q J 10 3 2
◊ K J 8
♣ A K 9

You reach 4♡ on an uncontested auction. West leads the ♠ Q. You have three sure losers and have to avoid losing a diamond. You can try a finesse in either direction or try for an endplay. The conditions are right; lots of trumps in both hands. Follow the play. Duck the opening lead and win Trick 2. Draw trumps.With trumps remaining in each hand, cash the ♣AK and lead a club.

You have reached this position:

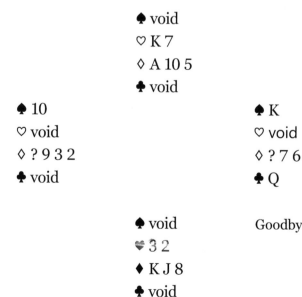

♠ void
♡ K 7
◊ A 10 5
♣ void

♠ 10   ♠ K
♡ void   ♡ void
◊ ? 9 3 2   ◊ ? 7 6
♣ void   ♣ Q

♠ void
♥ 3 2
♦ K J 8
♣ void

The opponents may have discarded differently but whoever wins the third club has to either play a diamond so no diamond problem, or play a black card, offering a ruff-sluff.

Goodbye diamond loser. In either case, making 4♡.

This deal shows an endplay in it's most basic form. We will show many variations, but the theme will remain the same.

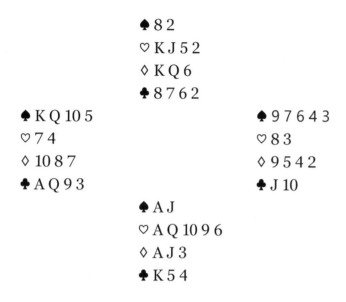

You reach 4♡ after West doubles your 1♡ opening bid and North raises to 2♡. West leads the ♠K. How should the play go? Win the opening lead and draw trumps. You need trumps to be 3-2 to have a trump remaining in each hand. This is a danger hand. You do not want East leading a club thru your king. But the opening lead has been helpful. Cash the diamonds, removing West's safe exit cards.

You have reached this ending:

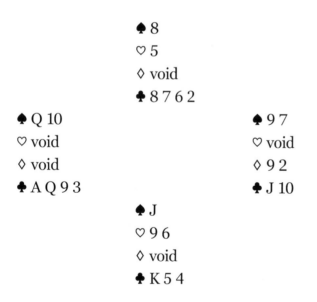

West wins but is endplayed. The best he can do is cash the ♣A. If South had tried leading a club to his king, he would have lost three clubs and a spade.

Suppose we change the previous deal slightly. Let's look at the spade suit.

♠ 8 6 3

♠ K Q 10 4   ♠ 9 7 5

♠ A J 2

The rest of the deal being the same, if West leads the ♠K, declarer cannot win the trick and play as before. If he later exits the jack, West can lead to East's nine. Then East will play a club.

Declarer must duck Trick 1. West cannot continue spades into the ♠AJ. Now declarer continues as previously. He later exits by playing first the ♠A, then the ♠J to complete the same endplay.

Another example of a little more work to be done.

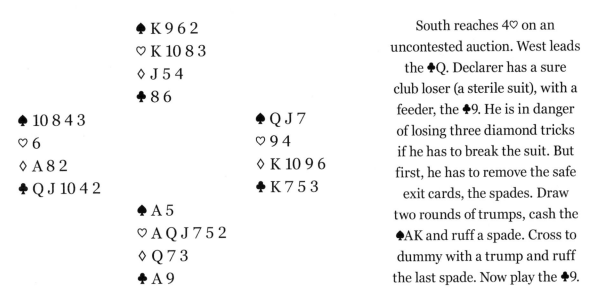

♠ K 9 6 2
♡ K 10 8 3
◊ J 5 4
♣ 8 6

♠ 10 8 4 3   ♠ Q J 7
♡ 6   ♡ 9 4
◊ A 8 2   ◊ K 10 9 6
♣ Q J 10 4 2   ♣ K 7 5 3

♠ A 5
♡ A Q J 7 5 2
◊ Q 7 3
♣ A 9

South reaches 4♡ on an uncontested auction. West leads the ♣Q. Declarer has a sure club loser (a sterile suit), with a feeder, the ♣9. He is in danger of losing three diamond tricks if he has to break the suit. But first, he has to remove the safe exit cards, the spades. Draw two rounds of trumps, cash the ♠AK and ruff a spade. Cross to dummy with a trump and ruff the last spade. Now play the ♣9.

Whoever wins the club is endplayed. Both opponents are void in hearts and spades. A club return allows a ruff-sluff. A diamond means declarer can only lose two diamonds by first just playing low.

One final example:

        ♠ A J 7 4
        ♡ A 5 3
        ◊ 7 6 4
        ♣ A 10 4

♠ 9   ♠ 10 5 2
♡ K J 8   ♡ Q 9 7 4
◊ J 10 9 8 3   ◊ A 5 2
♣ Q 7 6 5   ♣ J 8 2

        ♠ K Q 8 6 3
        ♡ 10 6 2
        ◊ K Q
        ♣ K 9 3

West leads the ◊J against South's 4♠. East wins and returns a diamond. Declarer has lost a diamond and has two sure heart losers. How can he avoid losing a club? He has no finesse position as the cards lie now. But let's see what can happen. Draw the trumps and cross to the ♡A. Ruff the last diamond and exit a heart. After the defenders cash another heart, it's club time.

Here is the position:

        ♠ J
        ♡ void
        ◊ void
        ♣ A 10 4

♠ void   ♠ void
♡ void   ♡ Q
◊ Void   ◊ void
♣ Q 7 6 5   ♣ J 8 2

        ♠ 8
        ♡ void
        ◊ void
        ♣ K 9 3

One defender will play a club. Play for split honors. If West leads the ♣5, play low. Capture East's ♣J with your king and finesse West for the queen. Just the opposite if East starts the clubs. Note that a good defender like you, if in this position, should start the suit by leading the honor and make declarer guess.

CHAPTER ONE

BASIC
ELIMINATION
DEALS

In this chapter, we will look at a variety of elimination and endplay deals.

The deals demonstrate a variety of techniques. There is no particular order to the deals.

The first few deals do demonstrate some basic classic positions.

1

DEAL 1. A CLASSIC

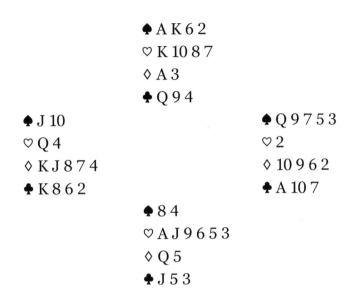

♠ A K 6 2
♡ K 10 8 7
◇ A 3
♣ Q 9 4

♠ J 10
♡ Q 4
◇ K J 8 7 4
♣ K 8 6 2

♠ Q 9 7 5 3
♡ 2
◇ 10 9 6 2
♣ A 10 7

♠ 8 4
♡ A J 9 6 5 3
◇ Q 5
♣ J 5 3

South opened a Weak 2♡ Bid on favorable vulnerability. North's 4♡ raise ended the auction. West led the ♠J.

Declarer won the opening lead and drew trumps. He made the right technical play in the club suit, leading low to his ♣J and later finessing dummy's ♣9. Tough luck. East won the ♣10 and ♣A, then shifted to the ◇10. When West covered South's ◇Q with the ◇K, declarer was down one.

Good opening lead, but could South have done better?

Yes. Remember what Dr J said about finessing? A last resort, not a first resort. Here South had a sure thing, a strip and throw-in.

The ♣9 is a black card but a red herring. A classic example of Qxx opposite Jxx. Whoever goes first in clubs loses a trick. After a spade lead, declarer should draw trumps, cash the other high spade and ruff a spade. Then cross to dummy with the diamond ace and ruff the last spade.

Now present the queen of diamonds to her consort and the unfortunate defender who wins will have to break the club suit. Whichever opponent leads a club, declarer plays low and is assured of a trick.

Making four hearts, losing only two clubs and one diamond.

DEAL 2. NO GUESS

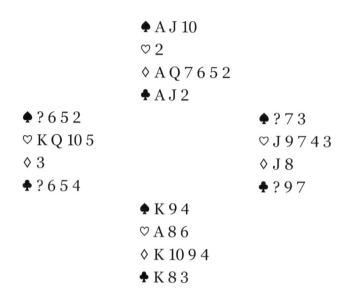

♠ A J 10
♡ 2
◊ A Q 7 6 5 2
♣ A J 2

♠ ? 6 5 2
♡ K Q 10 5
◊ 3
♣ ? 6 5 4

♠ ? 7 3
♡ J 9 7 4 3
◊ J 8
♣ ? 9 7

♠ K 9 4
♡ A 8 6
◊ K 10 9 4
♣ K 8 3

South opened 1◊ and judged well to avoid 3NT in favor of 6◊ despite having the ♡A opposite North's singleton.

West led the ♡K. South perused the dummy, knit his brow and said, "Columbus took a chance."

He won the ♡A, drew trump and finessed the ♣J. East won the ♣Q and exited in hearts. Declarer ruffed in dummy and led dummy's ♠J. When East followed with the ♠3 in tempo, South shuffled his spades face down on the table. We won't tell you which one he turned up, but he went down one.

"75% slam," said South as he scored up down one. "Half the time the club queen is on side. When it isn't I have a 50-50 chance of guessing spades right."

"Next time, try 'Eeny, meany, miney, moe,' in the spade suit," said North. "It works for me about 81% off the time."

Could you do better than 75% or 81%?

How about 100%? Instead of finessing in either black suit, ruff both low hearts in dummy, and exit with the ♣J after cashing both top clubs. Whichever defender wins the ♣Q will break spades for you. No guess.

DEAL 3. YOU'RE NOT TAKING ME

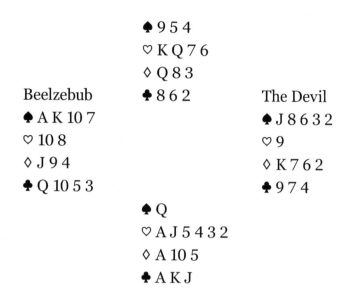

```
                        ♠ 9 5 4
                        ♡ K Q 7 6
                        ◊ Q 8 3
        Beelzebub       ♣ 8 6 2         The Devil
        ♠ A K 10 7                      ♠ J 8 6 3 2
        ♡ 10 8                          ♡ 9
        ◊ J 9 4                         ◊ K 7 6 2
        ♣ Q 10 5 3                      ♣ 9 7 4
                        ♠ Q
                        ♡ A J 5 4 3 2
                        ◊ A 10 5
                        ♣ A K J
```

You reach 4♡ on an uncontested auction. West tries to cash both top spades, but you ruff the second. The Devil is not above peeking in your hand, and whispers in your ear, "Don't sweat it. You're mine! I've got the king of diamonds and I'm sure my friend Beelzebub over there will hang on to his queen of clubs and jack of diamonds. He just loves that jack of diamonds."

Can you beat the Devil? All your finesses are going to hell.

Don't listen to that nasty fellow. You'll make the cold 4♡ so long as you take no finesses. Ruff dummy's last spade after taking the ♡A and ♡K. Then play clubs from the top to strip both black suits.

Turn to West, smile, and say, "Okay, Bub, you're in again. Let's see you get out. Well, what'll it be: ruff-sluff, or come to me in diamonds?"

In either case you will lose only one diamond trick no matter how the suit lies. Soon you will hear the dulcet tones of the Devil muttering "Curses, foiled again," as he slithers away.

DEAL 4. BASIC NOTRUMP ENDPLAY

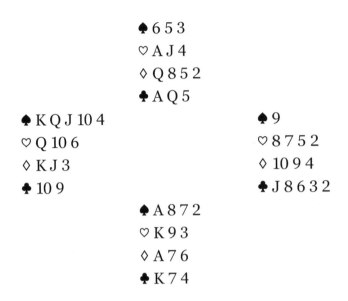

♠ 6 5 3
♡ A J 4
◇ Q 8 5 2
♣ A Q 5

♠ K Q J 10 4
♡ Q 10 6
◇ K J 3
♣ 10 9

♠ 9
♡ 8 7 5 2
◇ 10 9 4
♣ J 8 6 3 2

♠ A 8 7 2
♡ K 9 3
◇ A 7 6
♣ K 7 4

West opened 1♠ and after two passes, South bid 1NT, using a sensible 13-15 HCP range for balancing notrumps. North raised to 3NT.

Declarer ducked West's ♠K opening lead but captured West's ♠10 continuation with the ♠A. With the aid of a heart finesse, he won three heart tricks and three club tricks. He led the ◇A, hoping that the ◇K would fall beneath it. When the ◇A caught only the ◇J, South folded his cards and West claimed. Down one.

Wishful thinking. Can you see a much better play for nine tricks?

Again, let an opponent work for you. After cashing your hearts and clubs, stick West in with a spade. He'll take the rest of his spades, but at Trick 12 he'll have only ◇KJ left and have to give you your eighth and ninth tricks.

DEAL 5. TIMING YOUR ASSETS

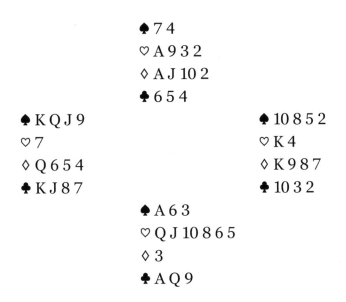

♠ 7 4
♥ A 9 3 2
♦ A J 10 2
♣ 6 5 4

♠ K Q J 9
♥ 7
♦ Q 6 5 4
♣ K J 8 7

♠ 10 8 5 2
♥ K 4
♦ K 9 8 7
♣ 10 3 2

♠ A 6 3
♥ Q J 10 8 6 5
♦ 3
♣ A Q 9

South opened 1♥. West doubled for takeout. North bid 2NT, "Jordan," the modern way to show a limit raise or better over an intervening double. South bid 4♥.

He won West's ♠K opening lead with the ♠A and lost a finesse to East's ♥K. East returned the ♣2. South deep-finessed the ♣9, losing to West's ♣J. West cashed the ♠J and exited with the ♠Q to tap dummy. Declarer had to lose another club at the end. Down one.

"Tough luck," sympathized North. "If only you'd had the jack of clubs instead of the nine, you could have made it."

Was North right? Would the nine of clubs have been enough for *you*?

Yes, if you knew to use it at the right time. The actual South let the opponents make him use it too early.

Let West hold the ♠K at Trick 1, keeping the safe hand on lead. Win the next spade and strip the hand to set the table for the endplay to come: ♦A and ruff a diamond. ♥A (no finesse, thank you!), ruff a second diamond, ruff your last spade and ruff dummy's last diamond.

Now for the main course. Feed East his ♥K. With your spades and diamonds gone, he must shift to clubs to avoid giving you a ruff-sluff. Cover his card, spread your cards, and claim your 4♥ game.

DEAL 6. FANCY BIDDING REQUIRES FANCY PLAY

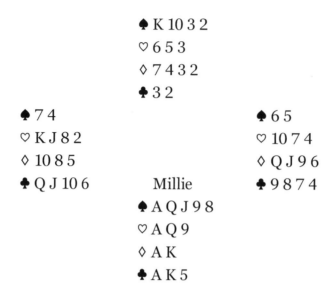

```
                    ♠ K 10 3 2
                    ♡ 6 5 3
                    ◇ 7 4 3 2
                    ♣ 3 2
      ♠ 7 4                         ♠ 6 5
      ♡ K J 8 2                     ♡ 10 7 4
      ◇ 10 8 5                      ◇ Q J 9 6
      ♣ Q J 10 6      Millie        ♣ 9 8 7 4
                    ♠ A Q J 9 8
                    ♡ A Q 9
                    ◇ A K
                    ♣ A K 5
```

Thoroughly Modern Millie won Danny in her local duplicate club's raffle at its Christmas party. "I've heard that you invent a new convention every morning before breakfast," she said. "I want to learn them all before our New Year's Eve game together."

"Are you drunk already?" asked Danny. Millie only smiled her most seductive smile. Danny blushed and sang "I'm just a boy who can't say no."

That's the only way we can explain how they reached 6♠ a week later via an Omnibus 2♣, Kleinish, Super-Marx and chutzpah. We'll show the auction marking conventional bids only with asterisks: 2♣*-2◇*; 3NT*-4♣*; 4NT*-5♡*; 5♠-6♠; pass. For explanations you'll have to ask Danny.

Alas, Millie's card play wasn't as sophisticated as her bidding. She won West's ♣Q lead, drew the ♠A and ♠K, lost a finesse of the ♡9 to the ♡J, and lost another finesse of the ♡Q to the ♡K. Down one.

How would you declare 6♠ to give yourself a better chance?

Win the ♣A, cash the ◇AK, lead to the ♠10, ruff a diamond, lead to the ♠K, and ruff the last diamond. Cash the ♣K and ruff the club.

With the minors eliminated and a trump still in each hand, lead a heart from dummy and cover whatever card East plays. West wins and is endplayed. Thank whichever god you believe in for good splits, and claim.

DEAL 7. NO ESCAPE

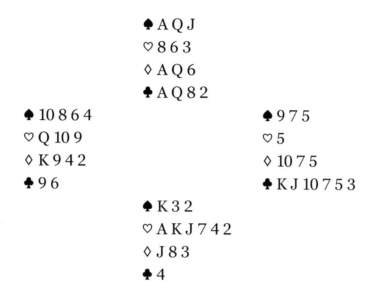

```
                    ♠ A Q J
                    ♡ 8 6 3
                    ◊ A Q 6
                    ♣ A Q 8 2
♠ 10 8 6 4                              ♠ 9 7 5
♡ Q 10 9                               ♡ 5
◊ K 9 4 2                              ◊ 10 7 5
♣ 9 6                                 ♣ K J 10 7 5 3
                    ♠ K 3 2
                    ♡ A K J 7 4 2
                    ◊ J 8 3
                    ♣ 4
```

Favorable vulnerability induced East to open a feathery 3♣ as dealer. North raised South's 3♡ overcall to 6♡. West led the ♣ 9.

Declarer won dummy's ♣A and cashed both top hearts, getting the bad news. Needing to catch the ◊K on side, he finessed the ◊Q. When it won, he cashed three spades and threw West in with a third trump. That could have worked if West had only diamonds left, but West exited with his last club (his last spade would have worked equally well) and declarer had no place to park his diamond loser. Down one.

South chose the right line, a strip and throw-in, but somewhere he got off the rails. Could you have stayed on track?

Not an easy deal, but upon learning of your trump loser, you can recover. Lead to dummy's ♠J and ruff a club, hoping that East preempted on a newly-fashionable six-bagger. When West follows, take two more spades in dummy and ruff another club. West dare not overruff for lack of a safe exit. He does better to pitch a diamond. Now you can finesse the ◊Q to reach dummy and ruff dummy's last club.

Poor West! Again he dare not overruff for lack of a safe exit, so he'll keep a guard for his ◊K and pitch his last spade. Now you've set the table and can feed West his trump trick. This time he's out of safe exit-cards and must lead from his remaining ◊K9. Note that if East had a normal 3♣ preempt (*seven* clubs), West could overruff early and exit safely in spades.

DEAL 8. DUMMY TURNS UP WITH A SURPRISE

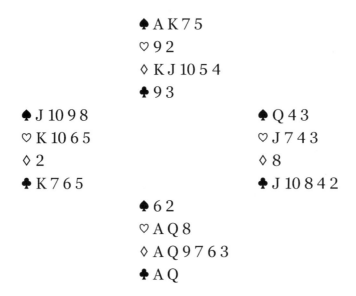

♠ A K 7 5
♡ 9 2
◇ K J 10 5 4
♣ 9 3

♠ J 10 9 8   ♠ Q 4 3
♡ K 10 6 5   ♡ J 7 4 3
◇ 2   ◇ 8
♣ K 7 6 5   ♣ J 10 8 4 2

♠ 6 2
♡ A Q 8
◇ A Q 9 7 6 3
♣ A Q

South opened 1◇ and rebid 2NT over North's 1♠ response. North's 4◇ jump showed great diamond support and slam hopes. South bid 6◇ directly. Well bid, gentlemen!

With some hope that she might score both kings on losing finesses, West led a safe ♠J.

Declarer won dummy's ♠K and drew trump with dummy's ◇10, unblocking the ◇9. Then he finessed the ♣Q.

West won the ♣K and exited in spades. South won dummy's ♠A and finessed the ♡Q.

West won the ♡K and South claimed down one. He murmured, "No finesse rapport! Either of two finesses: a 75 percent chance gone awry."

"Did you have the eight of hearts?" asked North, who had not seen the rest of South's hand.

Eight of hearts? What's that all about?

South was wrong about the 75%. The ♡8 in conjunction with dummy's ♡9 makes it 100%. Strip the spades and lead dummy's ♡9 (dummy's trumps provide extra entries). Cover East's card and claim. If West wins she can only give you a ruff-sluff or a free finesse.

DEAL 9. FROM THE OTHER SIDE

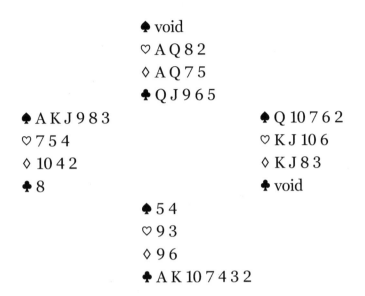

```
                    ♠ void
                    ♡ A Q 8 2
                    ◇ A Q 7 5
                    ♣ Q J 9 6 5
♠ A K J 9 8 3                          ♠ Q 10 7 6 2
♡ 7 5 4                                ♡ K J 10 6
◇ 10 4 2                               ◇ K J 8 3
♣ 8                                    ♣ void
                    ♠ 5 4
                    ♡ 9 3
                    ◇ 9 6
                    ♣ A K 10 7 4 3 2
```

West opened a classic Weak 2♠ Bid. North doubled. East visualized a good six-card spade suit and low doubletons in the red suits opposite. He placed both red aces with North for her double and thought West could make 5♠. Not relishing the prospect of South finding a cheap 5♣ save, he bid 5♠ directly. If South wants to sacrifice in clubs, let it be at the six-level!

South did, and East, with his well-stocked hearts and diamonds, doubled.

Declarer ruffed West's ♠K opening lead in dummy, drew trump with the ♣A and finessed the ◇Q. East won the ◇K and tapped dummy with a second spade. South returned to his hand with the ♣K and finessed the ♡Q. When it lost to the ♡K, he showed his hand and conceded down one.

"Another 75% slam down the drain," he muttered.

"Didn't we just have a deal like this?" groaned North. "How could you go down again?"

Yes, again it was a 100% slam after West led either black suit.

What was the most important card in South's hand? Again, the ♡9.

Strip the spades, lead another trump to hand, lead the ♡9 ... and claim!

DEAL 10. COUNT, COUNT, COUNT

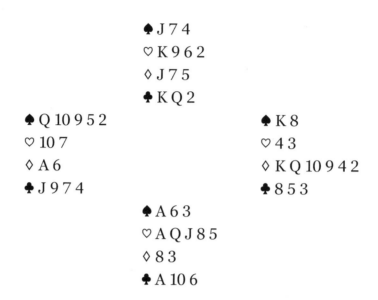

♠ J 7 4
♡ K 9 6 2
◊ J 7 5
♣ K Q 2

♠ Q 10 9 5 2   ♠ K 8
♡ 10 7   ♡ 4 3
◊ A 6   ◊ K Q 10 9 4 2
♣ J 9 7 4   ♣ 8 5 3

♠ A 6 3
♡ A Q J 8 5
◊ 8 3
♣ A 10 6

East opened a vulnerable Weak 2◊ Bid. South overcalled a non-vul 2♡. North raised to 3♡ and South bid was pleased to bid 4♡.

West led the ◊A and continued with the ◊6. East won and led a high diamond, which South ruffed high. Declarer drew trump in two rounds and led the ♠3, hoping for ... what?

Perhaps he was hoping that West had five spades to the ♠Q and would play her to keep dummy's ♠J from scoring. But West remembered his Mother Goose ("Second hand low!") and played the ♠10. East captured dummy's ♠J with the ♠K and returned the ♠8. South won the ♠A but had to lose another spade. Down one.

Could declarer have made 4♡ with better play?

Yes, had he stopped to think about East's distribution. After the first five tricks, declarer knew eight of East's cards (six diamonds and two hearts). By cashing three club tricks, declarer could learn more. When East follows to all three, declarer can place him with only one or two spades, almost surely ♠Qx or (more likely) ♠Kx for his vulnerable Weak 2◊ Bid.

Then lead the ♠A and duck a spade to East. With no spade to exit, East must offer a ruff-sluff. Bye-bye second spade loser, hello contract!

DEAL 11. DON'T GO FIRST

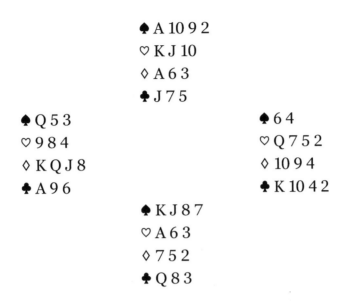

♠ A 10 9 2
♥ K J 10
♦ A 6 3
♣ J 7 5

♠ Q 5 3
♥ 9 8 4
♦ K Q J 8
♣ A 9 6

♠ 6 4
♥ Q 7 5 2
♦ 10 9 4
♣ K 10 4 2

♠ K J 8 7
♥ A 6 3
♦ 7 5 2
♣ Q 8 3

North opened 1♣ and raised South's 1♠ bid to 2♠, ending the auction.

West led the ♦K to dummy's ♦A. Declarer cashed dummy's ♠A and lost a finesse to West's ♠Q. West cashed two diamond tricks and exited with his last trump.

Declarer won, took the ♥A and lost a finesse of dummy's ♥J to East's ♥Q. East exited in hearts. The top clubs were split between the defenders, so declarer had to lose three clubs.

Unlucky? Unavoidable? Could you do any better?

Yes, by letting the defenders start as many suits as you can. Return a diamond at Trick 2. After taking two diamond tricks, West dare not lead his last diamond, as that lets you sluff from dummy and ruff in hand. But any shift blows a trick in the suit to which he shifts.

If he shifts to a trump, draw three rounds and start clubs. The defenders can take three clubs but must then break hearts.

If he shifts to hearts or clubs, you avoid a loser in that suit and can get rid of a loser in the other by playing spades from the top.

Any way you slice it, *two tricks saved.* Let the defenders do the work of breaking suits for you.

DEAL 12. YOU CAN'T GO DOWN UNLESS....

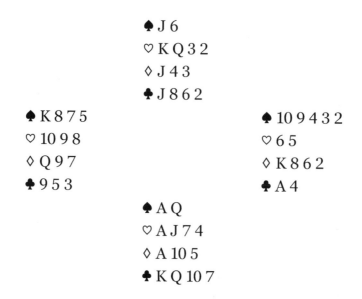

```
                    ♠ J 6
                    ♡ K Q 3 2
                    ◇ J 4 3
                    ♣ J 8 6 2
    ♠ K 8 7 5                      ♠ 10 9 4 3 2
    ♡ 10 9 8                       ♡ 6 5
    ◇ Q 9 7                        ◇ K 8 6 2
    ♣ 9 5 3                        ♣ A 4
                    ♠ A Q
                    ♡ A J 7 4
                    ◇ A 10 5
                    ♣ K Q 10 7
```

South opened 2NT and reached 4♡ via Stayman. He won West's trump lead with the ♡A, finished trumps with dummy's ♡K and ♡Q, and finessed the ♠Q.

West won the ♠K and returned the ♠5 to South's ♠A. South led the ♣K to East's ♣A and East returned the ♣4. Eventually, declarer had to break diamonds, and with the missing honors split he lost two diamond tricks. Down one.

"Another finesse, another loss," griped North. "Won't you ever stop?"

Another black queen, another red herring! The ♠Q is too valuable as a throw-in card to waste on an iffy finesse. Instead, start clubs. East may win and shift to spades, but now you can win the ♠A, cash all the clubs and throw a defender in with the ♠Q.

The defender who wins the ♠K must offer you a ruff-sluff or start diamonds for you. Either way, you lose only one trick in each suit except trumps.

DEAL 13. LOOKS GRIM BUT IT ISN'T

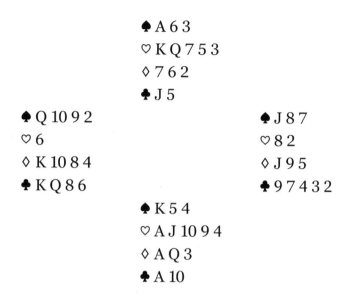

```
                    ♠ A 6 3
                    ♡ K Q 7 5 3
                    ◊ 7 6 2
                    ♣ J 5
  ♠ Q 10 9 2                        ♠ J 8 7
  ♡ 6                               ♡ 8 2
  ◊ K 10 8 4                        ◊ J 9 5
  ♣ K Q 8 6                         ♣ 9 7 4 3 2
                    ♠ K 5 4
                    ♡ A J 10 9 4
                    ◊ A Q 3
                    ♣ A 10
```

South opened 1♡ in fourth seat, and West doubled. North jumped to 2NT, the artificial but usual way for responder to show a limit raise or better over an intervening double. Dismissing any thought of slam opposite a passed partner, South settled for 4♡.

West led the ♣K. Mirror hand-patterns spell trouble. Despite his substantial extra strength, South saw four potential losers. He drew trump with the ♡A and ♡K, shrugged his shoulders, and finessed the ◊Q futilely. West won the ◊K, cashed the ♣Q, exited with the ◊10 and prayed for East to have the ◊J.

East obliged, and 4♡ went down.

"Did you ever meet a finesse you didn't like?" asked North.

Could South have made 4♡ by avoiding a finesse?

Yes. After drawing trump, cash both top spades and lead another. East may win and shift to diamonds. Forget the finesse, which is sure to lose on the auction. You don't need it anyhow.

Win the ◊A and lead the ♣10 to West's marked ♣Q. He'll be endplayed, able only to cash the ◊K or give you a ruff-sluff. You'll make 4♡.

DEAL 14. KEEP QUIET

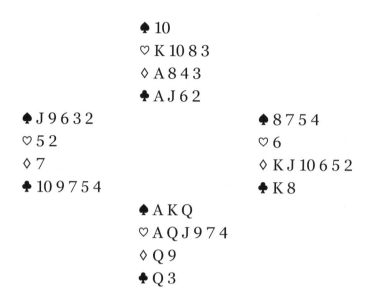

```
                    ♠ 10
                    ♡ K 10 8 3
                    ◊ A 8 4 3
                    ♣ A J 6 2
    ♠ J 9 6 3 2                        ♠ 8 7 5 4
    ♡ 5 2                              ♡ 6
    ◊ 7                                ◊ K J 10 6 5 2
    ♣ 10 9 7 5 4                       ♣ K 8
                    ♠ A K Q
                    ♡ A Q J 9 7 4
                    ◊ Q 9
                    ♣ Q 3
```

North and South were playing *Under-and-Over Splinters*, so instead of splintering with 3♠ (facilitating a sacrifice-suggesting double), North jumped to 4◊, just under four of his singleton (excluding the trump suit). Ironically, that let East double to show strong diamonds. South passed, letting North redouble to show the ◊A. After 4♠ and 5♣ cue bids, South placed the contract in 6◊.

West led the ◊7. Forewarned by the double, South feared a singleton. He won dummy's ◊A, drew trump and let the ♣Q ride for a finesse. East took the ♣K and ◊K. Down one, sure, swift, and wrong.

Without East's double, would you have played low at Trick 1?

Perhaps. Unless the ◊7 is singleton, 6♡ is cold after East wins the ◊K. Dummy's ◊A provides a club discard.

But the double of 4◊ draws a clear roadmap. You can win dummy's ◊A, draw trump and cash the ♠AKQ to discard two diamonds from dummy. Then lead the ◊Q to East's ◊K. East must give you either a free finesse in clubs or a ruff-sluff with another diamond or spade.

When Danny played chess as a boy, he would say "Zugzwang!" That means "You play, you lose!" (or "Endplayed!") in German. Though he loved the word, Danny always mispronounced it. But he never mispronounces "Silence is Golden" when he sings along with the Tremolos.

DEAL 15. GETTING THE KIDDIES OFF THE STREET

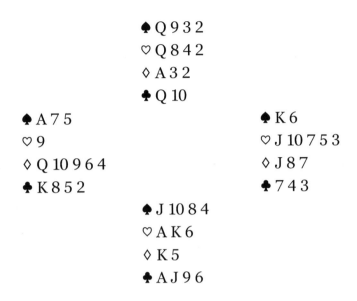

```
                    ♠ Q 9 3 2
                    ♡ Q 8 4 2
                    ◊ A 3 2
                    ♣ Q 10
    ♠ A 7 5                        ♠ K 6
    ♡ 9                            ♡ J 10 7 5 3
    ◊ Q 10 9 6 4                   ◊ J 8 7
    ♣ K 8 5 2                      ♣ 7 4 3
                    ♠ J 10 8 4
                    ♡ A K 6
                    ◊ K 5
                    ♣ A J 9 6
```

Though other routes were possible, South reached 4♠ via a mundane 1NT opening and Stayman.

West led the ♡9.

Declarer recognized a singleton when he saw one, so remembering having been taught to "get the kiddies off the street," he led the ♠4 to dummy's ♠Q promptly. East won the ♠K and gave West a heart ruff.

West cashed the ♠A and exited with the ◊10. Eventually South lost a club finesse and went down one. Seeing his partner shaking her head, he said, "I couldn't help it; I drew trumps as fast as I could."

Could *you* have helped it?

Well, yes. Sometimes speed kills. Drawing trumps quickly is often right but not always. Not when there is other work to be done first.

First you must remove West's safe exit. At Trick 2, cash the ◊K and ◊A then ruff a diamond to strip the suit. Only now is it time to take care of "the kiddies."

West will still get his heart ruff but after cashing the ♠A he'll have to offer you a ruff-sluff with a fourth diamond or a free finesse in clubs.

DEAL 16. AVOIDING DANGER

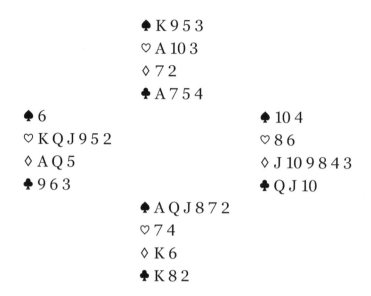

♠ K 9 5 3
♥ A 10 3
♦ 7 2
♣ A 7 5 4

♠ 6   ♠ 10 4
♥ K Q J 9 5 2   ♥ 8 6
♦ A Q 5   ♦ J 10 9 8 4 3
♣ 9 6 3   ♣ Q J 10

♠ A Q J 8 7 2
♥ 7 4
♦ K 6
♣ K 8 2

South opened 1♠ and North bid 4♠ directly over West's 2♥ overcall, minimizing the chances of the opponents finding a "favorable vulnerability" save.

Declarer captured West's ♥K opening lead with dummy's ♥A and saw sure heart and club losers. He realized that if he could keep East off lead, he might set up dummy's fourth club for a diamond discard. After drawing trump, he led a club from dummy, hoping to duck the first round to West.

But East played the ♣ 10. So much for Plan A. He tried Plan B, leading low to the ♦K. Down one.

North was sympathetic. "Nice try," she said. "Try to set up a second suit, first resort. When that fails, try a finesse. You must have read Dr J's book on the finesse as a last resort."

But was it really the last resort?

How about two other resorts, a loser-on-loser and an endplay? After drawing trump, cash two top clubs and stick West in with a heart, possible when dummy has the ♥10. When West plays a third heart honor, discard a club, a loser-on-loser.

Now West is endplayed. A fourth heart offers a ruff-sluff. A third club if West has one lets South ruff dummy's last club good. The ♦K must score.

DEAL 17. L O L

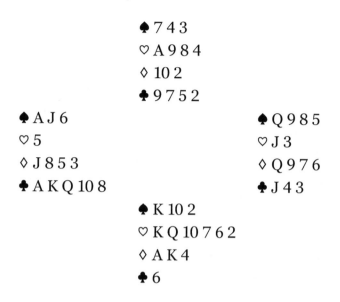

```
                    ♠ 7 4 3
                    ♡ A 9 8 4
                    ◊ 10 2
                    ♣ 9 7 5 2
    ♠ A J 6                         ♠ Q 9 8 5
    ♡ 5                             ♡ J 3
    ◊ J 8 5 3                       ◊ Q 9 7 6
    ♣ A K Q 10 8                    ♣ J 4 3
                    ♠ K 10 2
                    ♡ K Q 10 7 6 2
                    ◊ A K 4
                    ♣ 6
```

South opened 1♡ and West overcalled 2♣. North couldn't quite muster a 2♡ raise, but when South reopened with a takeout double, North strutted his stuff with a jump to 3♡ and South bid 4♡.

West led the ♣K, showing the ♣Q, and continued with the ♣A.

South ruffed and cashed the ♡K and ♡A. He ruffed another club, then cashed the ◊AK and ruffed a diamond. He led the ♠7 from dummy, hoping to cover East's card and endplay West. East played the ♠8 and West captured South's ♠10 with the ♠J. West exited with the ♣Q; South ruffed but lost two more spade tricks. Down one.

Was there any better line?

Yes. Declarer didn't have to touch spades. Instead, he could have led dummy's last club and discarded the ♠2, a loser-on-loser play.

Now West is endplayed.

DEAL 18. PUT THE OPPONENTS TO WORK

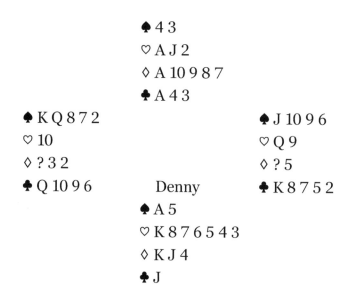

♠ 4 3
♥ A J 2
♦ A 10 9 8 7
♣ A 4 3

♠ K Q 8 7 2   ♠ J 10 9 6
♥ 10   ♥ Q 9
♦ ? 3 2   ♦ ? 5
♣ Q 10 9 6   Denny   ♣ K 8 7 5 2

♠ A 5
♥ K 8 7 6 5 4 3
♦ K J 4
♣ J

This deal shows Two-Over-One Game-Forcing at its best. After a game-forcing 2♦ response to 1♥ and a 2♥ rebid, North was able to bid a gentle 3♥. Now South had room to make a gentle 3♠ cue bid followed by a 4♦ cue bid after North cooperated with a 4♣ cue bid of his own. The cue bids in unbid suits promised aces, but South's 4♦, a cue bid in his partner's first-bid suit could be based on either the ♦A or the ♦K. North bid 6♥ without further ado. Well bid, gentlemen!

West led the ♠K to South's ♠A. South, Denny Decimal, knew his suit combinations, so he started trumps with his ♥K to cater to the 3-0 split he could handle, ♥Q109 with *West*. When West followed, South sighed with relief, for now he knew he had no trump loser. When East followed also, declarer drew the last trump with dummy's ♥A and started thinking about his next problem.

Well, dear reader, whom would you play for the missing ♦Q? What, you don't know? Neither do we. Denny stared at the ceiling, muttered something about "Finesse Rapport" and the "Theory of Empty Spaces," and misguessed. Down one, losing to the ♦Q and the ♠Q.

You don't need "Finesse Rapport" to bring this slam home, do you?

After both defenders follow to the ♥K, take the ♣A and ruff a club, cross to the ♥A and ruff another club. Then exit in spades. Whichever defender wins this trick must break diamonds or give you a ruff-sluff. Making 6♥, no guess and no finesse, thank you!

DEAL 19. A TALE OF THREE SIXES

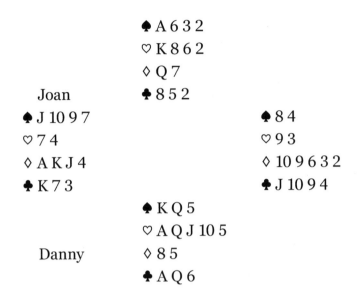

Joan
♠ J 10 9 7
♡ 7 4
♢ A K J 4
♣ K 7 3

♠ A 6 3 2
♡ K 8 6 2
♢ Q 7
♣ 8 5 2

♠ 8 4
♡ 9 3
♢ 10 9 6 3 2
♣ J 10 9 4

♠ K Q 5
♡ A Q J 10 5
♢ 8 5
♣ A Q 6

Danny

South opened 1♡ and Joan, West, made a takeout double. North raised to 2♡, avoiding the beginner's error of double-counting ♢Q7 as both a high card and a ruffing value. South bid 4♡.

West cashed both top diamonds and shifted to the ♡4. Declarer won the ♡J and ♡Q, then cashed three top spades ending in dummy. Had both defenders followed, he had planned to discard his ♣6 on dummy's ♠6 before trying the club finesse. Disappointed to see East discard the ♢6 on the third spade, declarer finessed the ♣Q. West won the ♣K and exited with the ♠J.

"My jack, please stay off it!" pleaded West. When declarer ruffed, she continued, "A gentleman would have let me score the jack of spades."

In the end, East took the setting trick with the ♣J. Danny, Southwest, shook his head sadly and said "Chivalry is dead. If I were declaring, Honey, I'd have given you the spade jack gladly."

Was Danny really chivalrous? Why would he have given Joan the ♠J?

In order to ensure the contract. When South discards the ♣6 on the ♠6 (loser-on-loser), West wins the ♠J and is endplayed. She must offer South a ruff-sluff or lead from her ♣K up to his ♣AQ. Zugzwang!

DEAL 20. LOCH LOMOND

```
                    ♠ A K J 4
                    ♡ A 10
                    ◇ A K Q 10 8 6
                    ♣ 6
♠ 2                                        ♠ Q 10 9 7
♡ Q J 6 5                                  ♡ 8 7 4 3
◇ 5                                        ◇ 4 3
♣ K Q 10 9 7 4 2    Lieutenant Dan        ♣ J 8 5
                    ♠ 8 6 5 3
                    ♡ K 9 2
                    ◇ J 9 7 2
                    ♣ A 3
```

North opened an Omnibus 2♣, the only powerhouse opening in his and nearly everyone's system. South bid 2◇, the usual neutral ("waiting") response with nothing else to bid. West bid 4♣, neither artificial nor waiting, North's 4◇ was the first natural bid for his side and South bid 6◇ forthwith.

Declarer won the ♣A at Trick 1, drew trump, cashed the ♠A and paused. "At matchpoints," he said, "I'd try a finesse for an overtrick. But at rubber bridge, I'll just play safe. I might catch a doubleton queen anyway."

He continued with the ♠K, commanding "Drop, queen!" as though he were still a drill sergeant in the army. Oops, West showed out.

"One last hope," said Lieutenant Dan. He tried the ♡A and ♡K, hoping the ♡J and ♡Q might fall. When they didn't, he ruffed the ♡9 in dummy. Then he came to his hand with the ◇J and led the ♣3.

West underplayed his carefully-preserved ♣2. Dan threw dummy's ♠4 and East's ♣J and ♠Q took the setting tricks. Any way to make 6◇?

Low Road: ruff a club at Trick 2, draw trump, ♡A, ♡K and a ruff a heart, ♠A and ♠4. East is endplayed.

High Road: after West shows out on the ♠K, come to the ◇J, ruff the ♣3, ♡A, ♡K and discard dummy's ♠4 on your ♡9. *West* is endplayed.

DEAL 21. JUST IN CASE

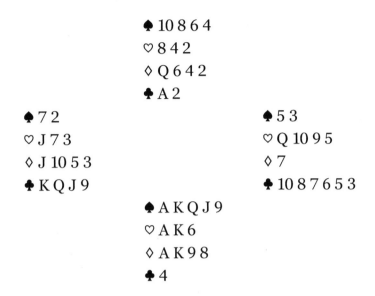

```
                    ♠ 10 8 6 4
                    ♡ 8 4 2
                    ◊ Q 6 4 2
                    ♣ A 2
        ♠ 7 2                      ♠ 5 3
        ♡ J 7 3                    ♡ Q 10 9 5
        ◊ J 10 5 3                 ◊ 7
        ♣ K Q J 9                  ♣ 10 8 7 6 5 3
                    ♠ A K Q J 9
                    ♡ A K 6
                    ◊ A K 9 8
                    ♣ 4
```

South opened an Omnibus 2♣ and rebid 2♠ over North's neutral 2◊ response. North's 3♠ raise showed values, so South had hopes for a grand slam. He bid a Roman Keycard Blackwood 4NT, and North's 5◊ reply told him that all the keys were present, but he had no way to learn whether North had the red queens that would warrant a grand slam. Nonetheless, South asked for specific kings with 5NT, confirming presence of all key cards, and passed North's king-denying 6♠ reply.

If there's a truly adequate way to bid the South hand, we haven't found it yet.

West led the ♣K. South did well to win dummy's ♣A and ruff a club to strip the suit. Then he drew trump, cashed both top hearts and exited with his last heart. East overtook West's ♡J with the ♡Q to shift to the ◊7, a *safe exit*. West's ◊J1053 sufficed to scuttle the good slam.

Good start, bad finish. South got to the basket but blew the layup. How would you have finished?

The only hazard is a 4-1 diamond split. To cater to this danger, South must cash the ◊A or ◊K before throwing the defenders in with a third heart. If the defender who wins started with four or five diamonds, no diamonds or one, his goose is cooked. Move over, Julius Erving: slam dunk!

DEAL 22. WILL THE REAL ENDPLAY SIGN IN?

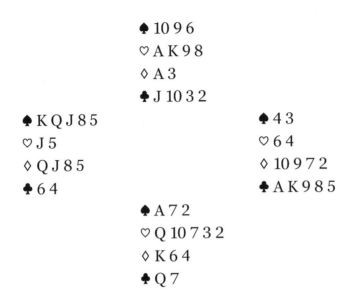

North opened 1♣ in second seat. South responded 1♡ and West overcalled 1♠. North and South had agreed to play "Support Doubles," so North's 2♡ raise promised four-card support. Counting his doubleton ♣Q at full value in light of North's club bid, South jumped to 4♡.

Declarer won West's ♠K opening lead with the ♠A and drew trump with dummy's ♡AK. He led low towards his ♣Q but East rose with the ♣K to return a spade. West won two spade tricks. East's ♣A took the setting trick.

Overbid? Maybe.

Unlucky? No, quite the opposite. Lucky that both top clubs were with East. Lucky that West had passed as dealer, marking him with only five spades when he hadn't been able to open with a Weak 2♠ Bid.

This deal occurred in a team game, and the only bad luck that this South suffered was having Danny as his East teammate in the other room. There South declared as recommended. Danny *ducked* when declarer led dummy's ♣2 to Trick 5. South won the ♣Q, stripped the diamonds, and led dummy's ♣J. Danny won the ♣K and ... zugzwang!

The overtrick cost an extra IMP and the match. "We won't invite *him* on our team again," said the team captain, who shall remain nameless.

DEAL 23. GOING DEEP

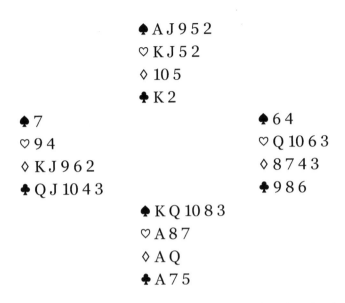

```
              ♠ A J 9 5 2
              ♡ K J 5 2
              ◊ 10 5
              ♣ K 2
  ♠ 7                        ♠ 6 4
  ♡ 9 4                      ♡ Q 10 6 3
  ◊ K J 9 6 2                ◊ 8 7 4 3
  ♣ Q J 10 4 3               ♣ 9 8 6
              ♠ K Q 10 8 3
              ♡ A 8 7
              ◊ A Q
              ♣ A 7 5
```

South opened 1♠. Not vul against vul, West bid an "Unusual" 2NT showing the two lowest unbid suits, a convention that is almost universal by now. North and South were using *TAUNT* ("Transfers Against Unusual No Trumps"), one of many counters to it. North's 3♡ showed *spade* support with game-try values or better.

East wisely refrained from bidding diamonds lest that induce West to lead from the ◊K or ◊AQ. South's 4♣ showed slam interest and the ♣A. When North bid 5♣, cooperating and showing the ♣K, South jumped to 6♠.

West led the ♣Q to dummy's ♣K. Declarer drew trump and tried to set up a third heart trick by dropping a short ♡Q. He cashed the **both top hearts** and led a third. East won and shifted to the ◊8. Down one.

Was there a better play for the slam?

Yes. Supposing West to have two hearts, by playing him for the ♡Q he gave himself only 6 chances in 15 to succeed (he succeeds also against ♡109 doubleton). But he'll double those chances, losing only when West has ♡64, ♡63 or ♡43 doubleton, by stripping the clubs, cashing dummy's ♡K, then leading dummy's ♡2 and covering East's card. Unless West has one of those three very weak doubletons, West will win and he'll be endplayed, forced to offer a ruff-sluff in clubs or a free finesse in diamonds.

DEAL 24. THE CURSE OF SCOTLAND

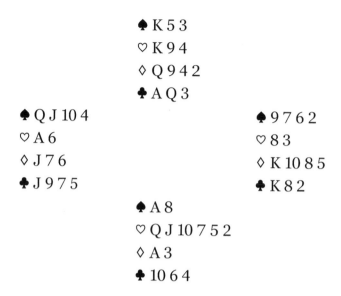

♠ K 5 3
♡ K 9 4
◊ Q 9 4 2
♣ A Q 3

♠ Q J 10 4   ♠ 9 7 6 2
♡ A 6   ♡ 8 3
◊ J 7 6   ◊ K 10 8 5
♣ J 9 7 5   ♣ K 8 2

♠ A 8
♡ Q J 10 7 5 2
◊ A 3
♣ 10 6 4

South responded 1♡ to North's 1◊ opening and placed the contract in 4♡ over North's 1NT rebid. He won West's ♠Q opening lead in hand, led to the ♡K at Trick 2, and continued with the ♡4 to his ♡Q and West's ♡A.

West continued with the ♠10 to dummy's ♠K. Declarer counted nine top tricks and saw two chances for a tenth in the form of dummy's two queens. First he tried diamonds, entering his hand with the ◊A and leading to dummy's ◊Q.

That finesse lost. East won the ◊K and returned the ◊5. South ruffed and finessed the ♣Q. That lost too. East won the ♣K and tapped declarer with a spade. West remained with the ♣J9 to ensure the setting trick.

Do you remember the subtitle of Dr J's book on "The Finesse"? *Only a Last Resort*. Must we make Gypsy Rose Lee a co-author to remind you?

Strip the spades early to deprive the defenders of safe spade exits. If West leads clubs, duck a low club or cover an honor; if he leads diamonds or you must break them yourself, win the ◊A first and lead the ◊3, covering West's card. East will win but be endplayed. A fourth spade offers a ruff and sluff. A club shift offers a free finesse. A diamond lets you discard two clubs while dummy wins one diamond. The ◊9 is *not* the Curse of Scotland.

DEAL 25. THE ERROR IN CULBERTSON'S HONOR TRICK CHART

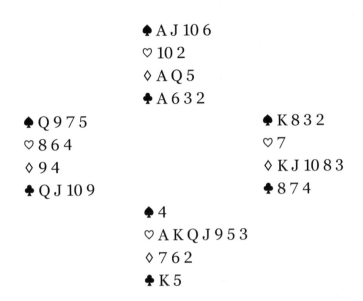

```
                    ♠ A J 10 6
                    ♡ 10 2
                    ◊ A Q 5
                    ♣ A 6 3 2
    ♠ Q 9 7 5                      ♠ K 8 3 2
    ♡ 8 6 4                        ♡ 7
    ◊ 9 4                          ◊ K J 10 8 3
    ♣ Q J 10 9                     ♣ 8 7 4
                    ♠ 4
                    ♡ A K Q J 9 5 3
                    ◊ 7 6 2
                    ♣ K 5
```

North responded 2♣ to South's 1♡ opening. That may seem strange to players who have been taught that 1♣, 1◊ and 1♡ openings all ask for unbid four-card majors. But especially when it is game-forcing, as it was for this pair, 2♣ is a much better response than 1♠, as it "relaxes" the auction. South jumped to 3♡ to show extras, here in the form of long, strong hearts.

Being unsure just how much extra South had, North jumped to 4♠, the "Kickback" convention that is best used to ask for keys when hearts are trump. Upon learning that ♠K and ◊K were missing, North settled for 6♡.

West led the ♣Q. South won the ♣K, led to dummy's ♠A and played dummy's ♠2 next, hoping that East might rise with the ♠K (or ♠Q with both) so he could knock out the other spade monarch to set up a twelfth trick.

No luck there, as East followed low. South ruffed, drew trump and finesse the ◊Q. No luck there either. He lost two diamond tricks: down one.

Any way to avoid relying on luck?

All the old textbooks from the Culbertson era show "Honor Trick" tables that list AQx as 1½, but AJ10 as only 1 and a "plus" value. That's wrong, as it understates the value of tens that bolster other honors. To avoid relying on luck, take the ♣K, ♡A and ♣A, then ruff a club high. Just to make sure East is out of clubs, cross to dummy's ♡10 and ruff another club high. Draw the last trump and deep-finesse dummy's ♠10. East can win but he's endplayed, and must lead up to dummy's ◊AQ or ♠AJ. Almost a lock!

DEAL 26. TOM SAWYER'S SECRET

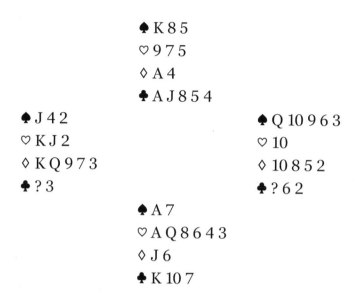

```
                          ♠ K 8 5
                          ♡ 9 7 5
                          ◊ A 4
                          ♣ A J 8 5 4
   ♠ J 4 2                                    ♠ Q 10 9 6 3
   ♡ K J 2                                    ♡ 10
   ◊ K Q 9 7 3                                ◊ 10 8 5 2
   ♣ ? 3                                      ♣ ? 6 2
                          ♠ A 7
                          ♡ A Q 8 6 4 3
                          ◊ J 6
                          ♣ K 10 7
```

South opened 1♡ on favorable vulnerability, and arrived at 4♡ after a leisurely game-forcing two-over-one cruise.

West led the ◊K to dummy's ◊A. Declarer finessed the ♡Q. West won the ♡K, cashed the ◊Q, and exited with the ♠2. Declarer captured East's ♠Q with the ♠A, but when the ♡J didn't fall on the ♡A next, he was left with a heart loser and had to guess the ♣Q to make.

Are you sure that West would overcall 2◊ if in addition to the high cards he's shown so far he had the ♣Q? Are you even sure that East has more clubs than West? Are you satisfied with 3-to-2 odds in your favor?

You know that in our books we never let declarers guess right. But do you know how to avoid the guesswork?

Tom Sawyer knew. Let your friends and neighbors—er, *opponents*—work for you. Lead to the ♡A at Trick 2. Strip the spades by cashing the ♠AK and ruffing one. The ◊J is a precious throw-in card. Offer it to West as if tendering a bribe. He'll surely win the ◊Q. Then sit back and watch him paint the fence for you. No matter which of the four suits he leads, one of your three possible remaining losers will disappear.

DEAL 27. NINE

```
                        ♠ 4 3
                        ♡ A J 10 7 3
                        ◊ K 8 2
      Mordecai Braun    ♣ A 7 3
      ♠ A Q J 8 7 5                    ♠ 10 9 6
      ♡ Q                              ♡ 5
      ◊ Q J 9                          ◊ 10 7 6 5 3
      ♣ K 10 2                         ♣ J 9 8 5
                        ♠ K 2
                        ♡ K 9 8 6 4 2
                        ◊ A 4
                        ♣ Q 6 4
```

The regulars at the Cavendish West Club feared the occasional large penalties inflicted upon Weak Jump Overcalls, especially at a nickel a point, but they hated old-fashioned Strong Jump Overcalls more. So most used Intermediate Jump Overcalls, part of "Cavendish West Standard."

West, Mordecai Braun, was glad to have one available when South opened 1♡ on Deal 4 (both sides vulnerable). He bid 2♠ and North bid 4♡.

South won the ◊Q opening lead with the ◊A, drew trump and stripped the diamonds. Knowing where the spades were, he led the ♠K, throwing West in with the ♠A. East dropped the ♠10.

"What did that show, Herr Braun: standard count?" asked South.

"Nein," answered Mordecai. Then he led the ♠5 and said "Finif."

East won the ♠9 and shifted to the ♣9. South tried the ♣Q, but West covered with the ♣K. Dummy's ♣A won but declarer had only nine tricks.

Could you have found a tenth?

Yes, if you'd let East in *before* West so you could throw West in later. After drawing trump and stripping diamonds, lead the ♠2. Let East's club shift ride to dummy's ♣A and then throw West in with his ♠A. Zugzwang!

DEAL 28. SIMPLICITY

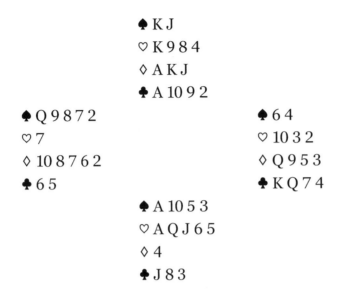

```
                    ♠ K J
                    ♡ K 9 8 4
                    ◊ A K J
                    ♣ A 10 9 2
    ♠ Q 9 8 7 2                      ♠ 6 4
    ♡ 7                              ♡ 10 3 2
    ◊ 10 8 7 6 2                     ◊ Q 9 5 3
    ♣ 6 5                            ♣ K Q 7 4
                    ♠ A 10 5 3
                    ♡ A Q J 6 5
                    ◊ 4
                    ♣ J 8 3
```

Playing Jacoby Forcing Raises, North responded 2NT to South's 1♡ opening, a demand for South to show shortness if he had any, or strength if not. South's 3◊ showed one diamond or none. Despite a redundant ◊K, North had values enough for 6♡. His 4♠ jump ("Kickback") asked for keys. South's 5♡ reply showed both missing aces and the ♡Q. North asked for specific kings with 5♠, and passed when South replied 6♡ to show none.

West led the ◊6 and South made an easy deal hard. He took the ◊K and drew trump. He cashed two top spades and ruffed a third. He threw the ♠10 on dummy's ◊A and ruffed off East's ◊Q.

Finally South let the ♣8 ride. When East won the ♣Q, South said "Endplayed!" and showed his hand.

"Not so fast," said East, "I have the nine of diamonds and I'm leading it. You can ruff but you'll have to give me my king of clubs in the end."

Down one. A lot of effort but no reward.

Could you have made this slam quickly and easily?

Sure. You have 10 top tricks and an eventual eleventh with a spade ruff in dummy. After drawing trump, let the ♣8 ride immediately. East can win, but then he's endplayed. His exit in any suit gives you a free finesse for a twelfth trick. Game, set, and match!

DEAL 29. FINESSE LEFT, FINESSE RIGHT, OR DROP?

♠ K 8 3
♡ J 3
◊ K J 7 2
♣ A 10 9 3

♠ A Q J 10 5 2
♡ void
◊ 6 4
♣ K J 7 4 2

We won't show you the East-West hands, but after East opens 1♡, South overcalls 1♠ and West raises to 2♡, a push-and-shove orgy finds East sacrificing in 5♡ on favorable vulnerability and South taking the push to 5♠.

West leads the ♡K. You ruff and draw trump with the ♠Q and ♠K. Perhaps surprisingly, both defenders follow twice. Most likely, East has both the ◊A and the ◊Q, so your contract appears to hinge on picking up clubs without loss. Or does it?

Finesse East for the ♣Q, finesse West for the ♣Q, or play for the drop?

Just to keep in practice, and perhaps because it might help, lead dummy's ♡J and ruff East's ♡A high. Now cash the ♣K, and when both defenders follow low, continue with a low club.

If West shows out, win dummy's ♣A and throw East in with his ♣Q. He'll be endplayed, forced to lead from his diamonds or lead a third heart, letting you ruff in dummy while dumping a diamond from your hand.

If West follows low, finesse! If East shows out, the clubs will run. If East wins the ♣Q, that's his last club, and he'll be endplayed just as in the case when he had ♣Qxx.

Finessing the other way risks defeat, for if West, the danger hand, gets in, his shift through dummy's diamonds will beat you.

DEAL 30. MULLIGAN WEEK IN HELL

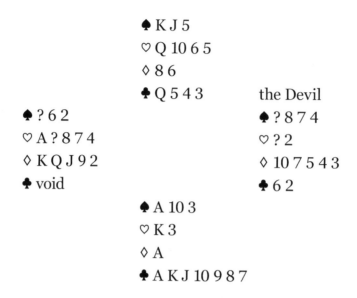

```
                    ♠ K J 5
                    ♡ Q 10 6 5
                    ◊ 8 6
                    ♣ Q 5 4 3        the Devil
    ♠ ? 6 2                          ♠ ? 8 7 4
    ♡ A ? 8 7 4                      ♡ ? 2
    ◊ K Q J 9 2                      ◊ 10 7 5 4 3
    ♣ void                           ♣ 6 2
                    ♠ A 10 3
                    ♡ K 3
                    ◊ A
                    ♣ A K J 10 9 8 7
```

When West's 1♡ opening came round to him, South doubled, as he was too strong to do anything else. North's 1NT advance showed values. Not knowing what else to bid (we don't know either), South gambled 6♣.

Declarer won the opening lead and drew trump with the ♣A and ♣J. He counted 11 sure tricks and pondered four plans for a twelfth: (a) finesse East for the ♠Q, (b) finesse West for the ♠Q, (c) finesse West for the ♡J; or (d) try to drop a doubleton ♡J in the East hand.

Figuring that East was devilish enough to hold the ♠Q despite West's opening bid, South tried Plan (a). Need we tell you it failed?

"It's Mulligan Week in Hell," said the Devil. "Take as many mulligans as you like. If all fail, of course, I'll take your soul."

South tried Plan (b). This time West had the ♠Q. Down one again. The Devil does have special powers. The same fate befell South when he tried Plans (c) and (d). Could you save your soul if you were South?

Yes, via a strip and endplay. At Trick 4, lead the ♡3. West must duck. Win dummy's ♡Q. Ruff the last diamond. Lead the ♡K to West's ♡A and cry "Zugzwang!" The Devil knows German and will concede 12 tricks.

DEAL 31. PICK YOUR VICTIM

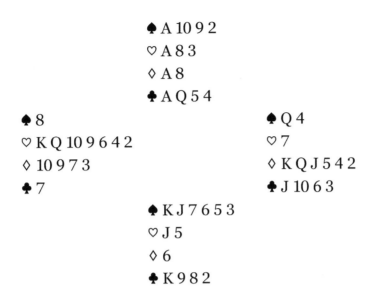

    ♠ A 10 9 2
    ♡ A 8 3
    ◇ A 8
    ♣ A Q 5 4

♠ 8   ♠ Q 4
♡ K Q 10 9 6 4 2   ♡ 7
◇ 10 9 7 3   ◇ K Q J 5 4 2
♣ 7   ♣ J 10 6 3

    ♠ K J 7 6 5 3
    ♡ J 5
    ◇ 6
    ♣ K 9 8 2

West opened 3♡ and North doubled. When South jumped to 4♠, North cue-bid 5♡ and South jumped to 6♠. West led the ♡K.

Declarer said "Good bid, partner, don't worry!" as he won dummy's ♡A. He drew trump with the ♠A and ♠K. When he played the ♣K and ♣A, West showed out. A bit flustered, South led to the ◇A and ruffed dummy's last diamond. Then he exited with the ♡J to West's ♡Q, knowing West had no club for safe exit. But West led the ♡10. Declarer lost a club at the end.

"I was trying for an endplay," said South. "All I needed was a third diamond play for a ruff-sluff."

"The right line of attack," said North. "But the wrong victim."

So, who was the right victim?

The defender who had no more hearts, of course. That could only be East. Did poor South forget which opponent had opened 3♡?

After winning Trick 1, drawing trump, stripping the diamonds and learning the bad news in the club suit, cash a third club and surrender the fourth. East must win and will be diamond flush. Away goes your ♡J while you ruff East's forced diamond exit in dummy.

DEAL 32. WE THREE KINGS (HEARTS)

♠ A Q 7
♡ J 8 6 2
◊ K 9 7
A 9 5

♠ 6 4
♡ A Q 7 5 4 3
◊ A Q J 10
♣ 7

South opened 1♡. Playing Jacoby Forcing Raises, North bid 2NT, showing values for 4♡ or higher and a balanced hand while asking opener for a singleton or void. South obliged with 3♣, and then the pair cue-bid adroitly. North's 3♠ showed the ♠A. South's 3NT was a waiting bid to encourage South to keep cue-bidding. North's 4 ♣ showed the ♣A. South's 4◊ showed the ◊A. North's 5◊ showed the ◊K, and that was enough for South to bid 6♡.

West led the ♣K. Declarer won dummy's ♣A and finessed the ♡Q. That lost. He ruffed West's ♣Q continuation, drew the last trump, and finessed the ♠Q. That lost too.

Do you see any better line of play?

There is one that is slightly better. If West has the ♠K, you can lose a trump trick and make 6♡ anyway, so assume that East has it. Consider a strip-and-endplay: ♠A, club ruff, ◊K and another club ruff, planning eventually to run diamonds and throw East in with his hoped-for bare ♡K.

Cashing the ♡A first gains when it drops a singleton ♡K in the West hand. Finessing the ♡Q first gains when West is void, for now you can continue with the ♡A to remove the guard from his ♡K. When he gets in, he'll be endplayed.

Any particular singleton is slightly more likely than a void. So laying down the ♡A gets the nod.

DEAL 33. WE THREE KINGS (SPADES)

♠ J 10 5 3
♡ 4
♢ A Q 7 5
♣ A Q 8 3

♠ A Q 9 6 4 2
♡ K Q 5
♢ 6 2
♣ 7 5

South opened 1♠. North and South were playing the usual form of splinter raises, in which 4♡ showed values for 4♠ or higher with a singleton or void in hearts. Aware of the duplicated heart values, South settled for 4♠.

West led the ♡J to East's ♡A and East returned a heart. Declarer won and tried three finesses in turn, each losing. 4♠ went down one.

"Seven to one odds against," griped South. "It could only happen to me."

Any way to get better than 7-to-1 odds?

Yes. If East has *any two* spades, you can make no matter where the minor-suit kings lie. After discarding dummy's ♢5 on the ♡K, cash the ♠A. If both defenders follow low, cash the ♡Q to discard dummy's ♣3. Then lead low to dummy's ♠10. If East has the bare ♠K left, he's endplayed and must give you a trick somewhere.

You'll lose when West is void in spades but gain when he has a singleton ♠K. Would you like us to say it again?

Any particular singleton is slightly more likely than a void.

DEAL 34. WE THREE KINGS (CLUBS)

♠ J
♡ A K 6
◇ A 9 8 4 2
♣ Q 9 6 4

♠ A 8
♡ 8 4
◇ K 5 3
♣ A J 10 8 7 5

When you play Two-Over-One Game Forcing and *Limit Raises* in the minors, as North-South here did, hands with which old-timers used to make forcing club raises are trouble hands. This pair played a 2◇ jump shift as an "FBI" catch-all for three strong hand types: *Fit, Balanced* or *Independent suit.* Any rebid other than in diamonds or notrump confirmed a club fit.

After South opened 1♣. North-South used "FBI" to cruise into 6♣.

West led the ♠K. When the club finesse lost, West cashed the ♠Q. Down one.

Did South give it his best shot?

No, the club finesse was only 50%. As a 2-1 split is a 78% shot, playing to drop a singleton ♣K offers a 26% chance, but another 52% of the time the ♣K will be doubleton. What South forgot was the losing to a doubleton ♣K is not always fatal, provided he strips the hand first.

Suppose he does: ♠A, ♡AK, heart ruff, spade ruff, ♣Q (East *might* cover with a guarded ♣K). If East plays a low club, however, win the ♣A. If West also plays a low club, however, a 52% chance, *it's not over.*

Continue with the ◇K, lead to the ◇A, and lead a club to whichever defender has the ♣K. He is a favorite *not* to have a majority of the missing diamonds ... and therefore to have to offer a ruff-sluff. That adds more than another 26% to the 2♣% chance of dropping a singleton ♣K.

Strip-and-Endplay noses out Finesse in this Derby.

DEAL 35. FAST REFLEXES

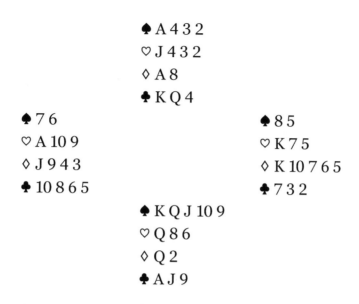

```
                    ♠ A 4 3 2
                    ♡ J 4 3 2
                    ◊ A 8
                    ♣ K Q 4
        ♠ 7 6                         ♠ 8 5
        ♡ A 10 9                      ♡ K 7 5
        ◊ J 9 4 3                     ◊ K 10 7 6 5
        ♣ 10 8 6 5                    ♣ 7 3 2
                    ♠ K Q J 10 9
                    ♡ Q 8 6
                    ◊ Q 2
                    ♣ A J 9
```

South opened 1♠ and North bid 2NT, which they played as an artificial forcing raise that denied a void. South alerted and was careful *not* to call it a "Jacoby Forcing Raise," for naming a convention is always wrong in explaining a call. Indeed, it *wasn't* "Jacoby," it was a "Boss Raise."

South rebid 3♠, the most discouraging rebid in his system, as it denied a void and denied lively slam interest.

A 3NT rebid (showing a heart void in his system) would have turned North on, and so would a 3♣ rebid (showing the ♣A and slam interest in his system) but 3♠ turned North off and he signed off in 4♠.

With little help from the auction, West guessed to lead the ◊3.

Without much thought South made the reflex play of the ◊8 from dummy, hoping to gain a trick if West had led from the ◊K. But East won the ◊K and returned the ◊6. Declarer lost three more tricks when he had to break hearts himself. Down one. Hearts, not diamonds, was the key

Would you have stumbled into the same pit as that poor soul?

We hope not. The deal is a virtual claimer. Rise ◊A, draw trump, clear clubs and feed the ◊Q to whichever defender has the ◊K. Zugzwang!

DEAL 36. YOU GET WHAT YOU DESERVE

♠ A 10 7 6
♡ K 3 2
◇ A 6 2
♣ J 6 3

Phil
♠ K Q J 9 8 5
♡ A J 4
◇ 3
♣ K 5 4

West opened a Weak 2◇ Bid and East raised to 3◇. South bid 3♠ and North raised to 4♠. West led the ◇J.

Declarer won dummy's ◇A, and ruffed a diamond high. He crossed to dummy's ♠A and ruffed another diamond high, then drew the last trump as West discarded a diamond.

South had nine sure tricks and saw three chances for a tenth: finessing West for the ♣A, finessing East for the ♣Q if East turns up with the ♣A, and finessing East for the ♡Q. Any one of these finesses will suffice if it works. Everyone get about 87½% for the chance of success?

South, Finessoholic Phil, tried all three. We're sure that having read this far in this book, you know his actual success rate was about 0%. Yes, West had ♠3 ♡Q105 ◇ KJ10975 ♣A82. He is allowed to have a maximum.

"Unlucky," moaned Phil. "If only I'd had *five* finesses to take, I'd have had a 96.875% chance. Von Wright's Law says that when you come *that* close to 100%, you're *certain* to succeed."

Did you take the 100% line, no finesses?

Very simple. Having stripped diamonds and spades, cash both top hearts and surrender the ♡J. Whoever wins must break clubs or give you a ruff-sluff. The most you can lose is two clubs and one heart no matter how the club or heart honors are divided.

DEAL 37. CLUELESS

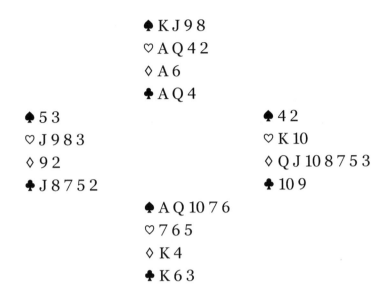

♠ K J 9 8
♡ A Q 4 2
◇ A 6
♣ A Q 4

♠ 5 3
♡ J 9 8 3
◇ 9 2
♣ J 8 7 5 2

♠ 4 2
♡ K 10
◇ Q J 10 8 7 5 3
♣ 10 9

♠ A Q 10 7 6
♡ 7 6 5
◇ K 4
♣ K 6 3

With East dealing at unfavorable vulnerability, South opened 1♠ out of turn. West, perhaps fearing that if given the chance East might open and get into trouble, condoned it.

"No harm, no foul," said North as he bid 2NT, which he played as a Jacoby Forcing Raise. South, with no shortness and no extras, jumped to 4♠, part of the "Jacoby Forcing Raise" convention called "FAST" (no, not named for Howard Fast, most famous for his novel *Spartacus*, but an acronym for "Fast Arrival Shows Trash").

West led a passive ◇9.

Declarer counted 11 top tricks. He drew trump, stripped both minors just to keep in practice, and finessed the ♡Q. No luck. East won the ♡K and exited with the ♡10. West hung on to his hearts, and South finished with the same 11 tricks he counted initially.

Could you have found that elusive twelfth trick?

Maybe. After drawing trump and before stripping the minors, cash the ♡A. Can't hurt! A second-round finesse will do just as well as a first-round finesse when the ♡K is on side. Then lead towards the ♡Q. East will still win the ♡K but have to exit in diamonds, giving you a ruff-sluff.

DEAL 38. DID FINESSOHOLIC PHIL
EVER MISS A FINESSE?

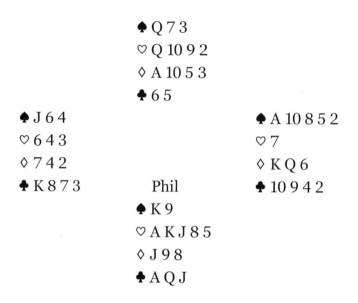

```
                    ♠ Q 7 3
                    ♡ Q 10 9 2
                    ◇ A 10 5 3
                    ♣ 6 5
    ♠ J 6 4                        ♠ A 10 8 5 2
    ♡ 6 4 3                        ♡ 7
    ◇ 7 4 2                        ◇ K Q 6
    ♣ K 8 7 3      Phil            ♣ 10 9 4 2
                    ♠ K 9
                    ♡ A K J 8 5
                    ◇ J 9 8
                    ♣ A Q J
```

West led a passive ♡4 after a routine 1♡-2♡-4♡ auction. South opened 1♡ and bid 4♡ after North raised. West led the ♡ 3.

Lots of finesses! Declarer won Trick 1 with dummy's ♡9 and lost Finesse #1, as his ♣Q fell to West's ♣K. He won the trump return and lost Finesse #2, as his ◇J rode to East's ◇Q. He won the club return, drew the last trump, and lost Finesse #3, as his ◇9 rode to East's ◇K. Zero for three.

"You love finesses, don't you?" asked East. "Guess I better cash this before you finesse me out of it," he continued, thumbing the ♠A on the table. Down one.

"Did you ever see a finesse that you didn't like?" asked North rhetorically in the post-mortem.

Well, did he?

Yes! Upon winning the second heart, South might have finessed successfully against East's ♠A. If East played it on air, dummy's ♠Q would eventually provide declarer's tenth trick. So East would have to play low.

Now declarer can draw the last trump, cash the ♣A and ♣J to discard a spade from dummy and throw East in with the ♠Q. Zugzwang! East must either break diamonds or give a ruff-sluff.

40

DEAL 39. NOTHING FANCY, THANK YOU

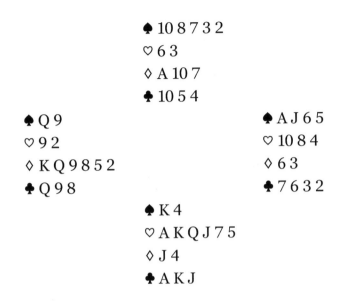

♠ 10 8 7 3 2
♡ 6 3
♢ A 10 7
♣ 10 5 4

♠ Q 9
♡ 9 2
♢ K Q 9 8 5 2
♣ Q 9 8

♠ A J 6 5
♡ 10 8 4
♢ 6 3
♣ 7 6 3 2

♠ K 4
♡ A K Q J 7 5
♢ J 4
♣ A K J

South opened a shaded Omnibus 2♣ on favorable vulnerability. After a neutral 2♢ response and South's 2♡ rebid, North bid a negative 2NT. No fancy "three clubs negative" for her! Not only would a negative 3♣ keep responder from rebidding 3♣ as a natural positive, it would also keep opener from making a natural 3♣ rebid with a heart-club two-suiter.

South rebid 3♡ to show a sixth heart. North, happy to learn that they had eight between them, raised to 4♡.

West led the ♢K. Declarer counted only nine top tricks but saw that dummy's ♢10 would be a tenth. Trouble was, if he won the ♢A, drew trump and led the ♢J to drive out West's ♢Q, he would have no way to reach dummy to cash the ♢10.

Suddenly he remembered a bridge book he'd read recently: *An Entry, an Entry, My Kingdom for an Entry*. He wished he remembered the authors' names so he could thank them. He played low from dummy and unblocked the ♢J. West continued the ♢8. Triumphantly, declarer finessed dummy's ♢10. Then he cashed—oops, no, East ruffed—dummy's ♢A. He overruffed and drew trump, but suddenly he was back down to nine tricks. Down one.

Any way to make 4♡? Sure. Via an endplay. Win the ♢A, draw trump, lead the ♢J to West's ♢Q and voila, any exit by West gives him a tenth trick.

DEAL 40. A LITTLE L O L CAN'T HURT

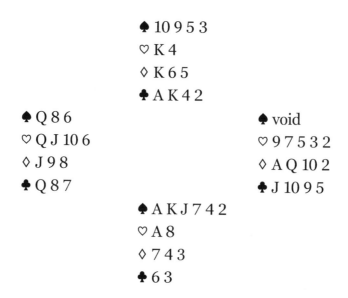

```
                    ♠ 10 9 5 3
                    ♡ K 4
                    ◊ K 6 5
                    ♣ A K 4 2
♠ Q 8 6                              ♠ void
♡ Q J 10 6                           ♡ 9 7 5 3 2
◊ J 9 8                              ◊ A Q 10 2
♣ Q 8 7                              ♣ J 10 9 5
                    ♠ A K J 7 4 2
                    ♡ A 8
                    ◊ 7 4 3
                    ♣ 6 3
```

South opened 1♠ and with neither shortness nor substantial extra strength, he made a "Fast Arrival Shows Trash" jump to 4♠ over North's 2NT Jacoby Forcing Raise.

Upon winning West's ♡Q opening lead with the ♡A and cashing the

♠A, South found he had a trump loser. He cashed the ♠K and led to dummy's ◊K, losing to the ◊A. Unlucky! Two more diamond losers meant down one.

Any way to recover from the unfavorable spade break?

At least try. After cashing both top trumps, try for a strip and endplay. Cash the ♣AK and ruff a club. Cross to the ♡K and lead the last club. When East, the safe hand covers, discard a diamond, *loser-on-loser*.

East is endplayed. A diamond return gives you a diamond trick and a heart gives you a ruff-sluff.

With West having three spades and East having none, East is a favorite to have four clubs. But if not, you've lost nothing. The diamond finesse is still available as a last resort.

DEAL 41. FINESSE YOU LOSE, NO FINESSE YOU WIN

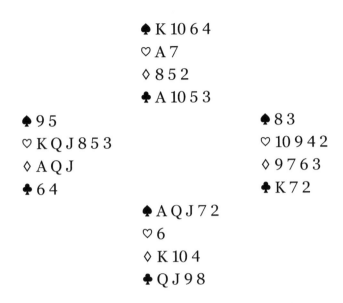

♠ K 10 6 4
♡ A 7
◇ 8 5 2
♣ A 10 5 3

♠ 9 5
♡ K Q J 8 5 3
◇ A Q J
♣ 6 4

♠ 8 3
♡ 10 9 4 2
◇ 9 7 6 3
♣ K 7 2

♠ A Q J 7 2
♡ 6
◇ K 10 4
♣ Q J 9 8

South opened 1♠ and West overcalled 2♡. North cue-bid 3♡ to show a forcing raise and settled for 4♠ when South made no try for slam.

West led the ♡K to dummy's ♡A. Declarer drew trump and let the ♣Q ride to East's ♣K. He ducked East's ◇7 shift to West's ◇J and ruffed West's ♡J exit. He finished clubs but remained with two more diamond losers. Down one.

Could you have reduced the four apparent losers to three?

Yes, if you could remove West's safe exit cards. A good move is to strip the hearts by ruffing a heart at Trick 2. That removes one of West's out-cards. Then, after drawing trump, remove another of West's out-cards by cashing dummy's ♣A.

Now you can lead the ♣K. If West wins the ♣K and leads another club, you can finish clubs ending in dummy and lead a diamond, covering East's card, endplaying West to hold your diamond losers to two.

You'll fail only if West started with three low clubs and can exit in clubs after winning East's diamond shift. But in that case, the club finesse couldn't help you anyway.

DEAL 42. THE SYMPATHETIC HUSBAND

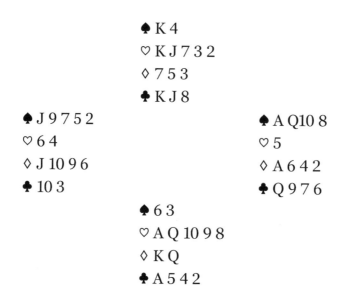

```
                    ♠ K 4
                    ♡ K J 7 3 2
                    ◇ 7 5 3
                    ♣ K J 8
  ♠ J 9 7 5 2                      ♠ A Q10 8
  ♡ 6 4                            ♡ 5
  ◇ J 10 9 6                       ◇ A 6 4 2
  ♣ 10 3                           ♣ Q 9 7 6
                    ♠ 6 3
                    ♡ A Q 10 9 8
                    ◇ K Q
                    ♣ A 5 4 2
```

After a 1♡ - 3♡ - 4♡ auction, West led the ◇J.

East won the ◇A and returned the ◇2. Declarer drew trump ending in hand and led the ♣2 to West's ♣3 and dummy's ♣J. East won the ♣Q and tapped declarer in diamonds. Declarer ruff and cashed the ♣K and ♣A.

When clubs split 4-2, she led to the ♠K. That finesse lost too. Two spade losers plus one loser in each minor meant down one.

"Good thing there were no more finesses available for you to take, dear, or you might have gone down more," said North, South's sympathetic husband.

We can commend North for his kindness, but was he right?

No, he was wrong on three counts. There *was* another finesse available, South *didn't* take it, and if she had taken it she'd have *made* 4♡.

After winning Trick 2, cross to dummy in trump and ruff dummy's last diamond. Cash the ♡A and lead the ♣2. When West plays the ♣3, *deep*-finesse dummy's ♣8. East can win the ♣9 but is endplayed in three suits. Rising with the ♣10 wouldn't help West, as then playing dummy's ♣J produces the same endplay.

DEAL 43. FINESSE? NO, CREATE AN ENDPLAY

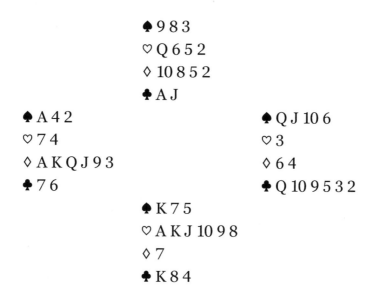

$\spadesuit$ 9 8 3
$\heartsuit$ Q 6 5 2
$\diamondsuit$ 10 8 5 2
$\clubsuit$ A J

$\spadesuit$ A 4 2
$\heartsuit$ 7 4
$\diamondsuit$ A K Q J 9 3
$\clubsuit$ 7 6

$\spadesuit$ Q J 10 6
$\heartsuit$ 3
$\diamondsuit$ 6 4
$\clubsuit$ Q 10 9 5 3 2

$\spadesuit$ K 7 5
$\heartsuit$ A K J 10 9 8
$\diamondsuit$ 7
$\clubsuit$ K 8 4

South opened 1$\heartsuit$ and West overcalled 2$\diamondsuit$. North bid 2$\heartsuit$ and South gambled 4$\heartsuit$.

West led and continued high diamonds. South ruffed and cashed both top trumps. Fearing that West had the $\spadesuit$A for his overcall (but we'd surely have bid the same with $\spadesuit$Q102 instead, wouldn't you?), South thought to avoid a spade finesse. We sympathize.

Clubs offered an alternative. A finesse against West's possible $\clubsuit$Q could provide a discard for a spade loser and a tenth trick. That finesse lost (don't they all in this book?). South went down two, losing three spades, one club, and one diamond.

Good operation, but the patient died. Do you see a better surgery?

East is the danger hand, and a *minorectomy* will keep him off lead. After drawing trump, lead to the $\clubsuit$A and ruff another diamond. Cash the $\clubsuit$K and ruff your last club. Then pitch a spade on dummy's $\diamondsuit$10, *loser-on-loser*. West will win and be endplayed, forced to offer a ruff-sluff or break spades.

This operation has a 0.00% failure rate.

DEAL 44. LOTS OF INFORMATION

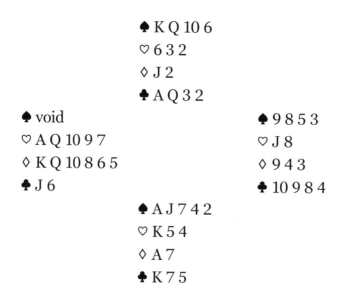

      ♠ K Q 10 6
      ♡ 6 3 2
      ◊ J 2
      ♣ A Q 3 2

♠ void   ♠ 9 8 5 3
♡ A Q 10 9 7   ♡ J 8
◊ K Q 10 8 6 5   ◊ 9 4 3
♣ J 6   ♣ 10 9 8 4

      ♠ A J 7 4 2
      ♡ K 5 4
      ◊ A 7
      ♣ K 7 5

Though in range for 1NT, South did well to open in his five-card spade suit, as his system let him rebid 2NT over a 2♣ or 2◊ response to show a hand like his.

West's 2♠ was Specific Michaels, a version that showed the two top unbid suits. Against that North-South played 3♣ and 3♠ as natural and invitational while 3◊ and 3♡ were artificial and forcing in the lower and higher of the other two suits respectively. North strained to bid 3♡ and signed off in 4♠ next.

South captured West's ◊K opening lead with the ◊A and faced four possible losers, as West undoubtedly had the ♡A. He drew trump, needing four pulls, and tried for 3-3 clubs, but the 4-2 split held him to nine tricks.

The auction and early play provided lots of information; could you have put it to better use?

Yes. Upon discovering the 4-0 spade split, test clubs immediately. When West shows out on the third club, throw him in with his ◊Q. He must either break hearts for you or continue diamonds, letting you ruff in dummy while shedding a heart from your hand. Ten tricks any way you slice it.

DEAL 45. AFTER YOU, PLEASE

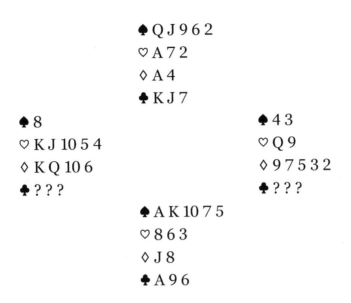

```
                    ♠ Q J 9 6 2
                    ♡ A 7 2
                    ◊ A 4
                    ♣ K J 7
        ♠ 8                       ♠ 4 3
        ♡ K J 10 5 4              ♡ Q 9
        ◊ K Q 10 6               ◊ 9 7 5 3 2
        ♣ ? ? ?                   ♣ ? ? ?
                    ♠ A K 10 7 5
                    ♡ 8 6 3
                    ◊ J 8
                    ♣ A 9 6
```

North and South were using Jacoby Forcing Raises. North's 2NT response to 1♠ showed a balanced forcing raise. South's "Fast Arrival" 4♠ jump showed a balanced minimum, foreclosing any slam tries below game.

West led the ◊K. South saw the mirrored distribution with three sure losers in the red suits and a possible club loser. He drew trump with the ♠K and ♠Q, then led to the ♣A and finessed the ♣J, a 50% chance.

In this book 50% chances fail. But 75% chances often succeed. Yogi Berra once tried to do the math. He said, "90% of the time, 75% chances come home. The other third of the time they get thrown out at third base."

Who could argue with Yogi? The actual South did. Gil McDougald was waiting for him at third base and supplied the tag with the ♣Q.

The 75% play? At Trick 4, lead to the ◊J. West must win and will do best to shift to the ♡J. Win the ♡A, burn a trump entry to your hand and lead another heart. West will win the ♡10—oops, no! East will overtake with the ♡Q perforce and be endplayed. A Crocodile Coup!

Only if West rises with the ♡K and cashes the ♡10 next will he be able to shift to clubs, and only when East has both ♣Q and ♣10 will 4♠ fail.

Yogi was right. In theory, a 75% play, but in practice, 90%. Sorry, Gil.

DEAL 46. ANNOYING

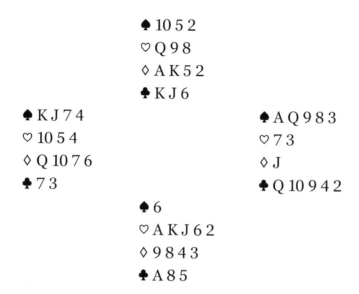

        ♠ 10 5 2
        ♡ Q 9 8
        ◇ A K 5 2
        ♣ K J 6

♠ K J 7 4   ♠ A Q 9 8 3
♡ 10 5 4   ♡ 7 3
◇ Q 10 7 6   ◇ J
♣ 7 3   ♣ Q 10 9 4 2

        ♠ 6
        ♡ A K J 6 2
        ◇ 9 8 4 3
        ♣ A 8 5

South opened 1♡. North bid 2◇, forcing to game in his methods. Undaunted, East doubled in hopes of finding a profitable sacrifice. West competed with 3♠ over South's 3◇ raise, but East, having given his all when he doubled 2◇, sold out to North's 4♡.

West led the ♠4 to East's ♠A. South ruffed East's ♠8 return and sighed with relief when both defenders followed to the ♡A and ♡J. South left one trump outstanding and cashed both of dummy's top diamonds.

Declarer read East for a 5=2=1=5 hand from the auction. When East showed out, declarer thought to cash both top clubs and throw East in with the ♣Q to get a ruff-sluff for her tenth trick. Alas, an alert West ruffed in with the ♡10 and cashed two diamond honors for down one.

Declarer was on the right track, but got sidetracked. Any suggestions for getting back on track to make?

A partial elimination and endplay is the right idea. But to carry it out, declarer must ruff dummy's last spade. She can use dummy's ♡Q as an entry to do this, so after ruffing the second spade, she can take the ♡K and dummy's ♡Q to ruff a third spade. Now the best play is ducking a diamond to East. After winning his singleton ◇J, East is endplayed.

A club exit runs to dummy's ♣KJ6 and a fourth spade lets declarer shed a diamond and ruff in dummy. Either way, ten tricks.

DEAL 47. THE RAGGEDY RABBIT'S FOOT

♠ A 10 7 6 2
♡ K 9 3
♦ A Q 3
♣ 7 6

♠ K Q 9 8 4
♡ A 10 2
♦ K 7 2   Sue Ellen
♣ A 4

Having been told, "If it looks like a duck, waddles like a duck, and quacks like a duck, it's a notrump opening," South opened this distinctly non-notrumpish hand 1NT instead of a sensible 1♠. He made up for it by jump-accepting North's Jacoby Transfer. North invoked Roman Keycard Blackwood and stopped in 6♠ upon learning of the missing ♣K.

West led the ♣Q. South won the ♣A and drew trump. He drew a well-worn rabbit's foot from a pocket and rubbed it for exactly seven seconds. Then he cashed both top hearts, hoping to drop ♡QJ doubleton in either defender's hand. Not today, down one.

He turned to Sue Ellen, his admiring right-hand kibitzer, and said, "My birthday is coming in three weeks. Don't you think a new rabbit's foot would make a useful present?"

No, Sue Ellen should not buy him a new rabbit's foot. A new bridge book (this one!) would be a more useful present. Playing to drop ♡QJ doubleton offers about a 5% chance, A strip-and-endplay offers about a 50% chance.

After drawing trump, strip the diamonds and exit in clubs. To avoid giving a ruff-sluff, the defender who wins must shift to hearts. Play for split honors. If he shifts to a low heart, let it ride, capture his partner's honor, and finesse him for the other honor.

What should you do if the winner of the club trick shifts to a heart honor?

That's his best play, as it gives you a losing option.

Cover, and then finesse the other defender for the other honor. Do not let an opponent derail you from the right track. If the winner of the club trick had both missing heart honors, don't you think he'd have let his partner win the club?

DEAL 48. THE GIRLS IN THE OTHER ROOM

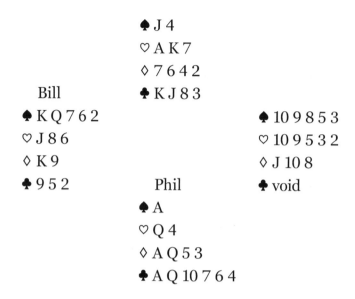

```
                          ♠ J 4
                          ♡ A K 7
                          ◊ 7 6 4 2
            Bill          ♣ K J 8 3
        ♠ K Q 7 6 2                      ♠ 10 9 8 5 3
        ♡ J 8 6                          ♡ 10 9 5 3 2
        ◊ K 9                            ◊ J 10 8
        ♣ 9 5 2          Phil            ♣ void
                          ♠ A
                          ♡ Q 4
                          ◊ A Q 5 3
                          ♣ A Q 10 7 6 4
```

South opened 1♣. West overcalled 1♠. North didn't much value his doubleton ♠J and settled for a sound 3♣ limit raise. When South cue-bid 3♠, they were off to the races. North cue-bid 4♡ and South bid 6♣.

West led the ♠K against 6♣. Declarer won and drew trumps. He finessed the ◊Q, losing to West's ◊K. He ruffed West's ♠Q next and discarded one of his two low diamonds on the hearts but had to lose another low diamond at the end. Down one.

This deal occurred in a friendly team game among four married couples. Richard, North, was the first to speak in the post-mortem.

"Shoulda made it, Phil. Wild Bill's overcall and king-lead gave it away.

Draw trump, pitch a diamond on the hearts, pitch another diamond on the jack of spades and give Bill his queen. He'll be endplayed: ruff-sluff or lead to your bare ace-queen. You'll get by with a little help from your friends."

"No swing," said Phil. "In the other room, my Cora is West. She won't overcall and she leads trumps against slams. Kate will go down too."

Did these men know their wives?

Yes and no. Cora passed throughout and led the ♣5. But Kate played as Richard suggested and made 6♣. It was the best line regardless.

DEAL 49. TIE-BREAKERS

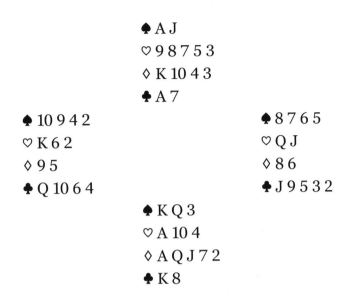

        ♠ A J
        ♡ 9 8 7 5 3
        ◊ K 10 4 3
        ♣ A 7

♠ 10 9 4 2   ♠ 8 7 6 5
♡ K 6 2   ♡ Q J
◊ 9 5   ◊ 8 6
♣ Q 10 6 4   ♣ J 9 5 3 2

        ♠ K Q 3
        ♡ A 10 4
        ◊ A Q J 7 2
        ♣ K 8

South opened 1◊ and rebid 2NT over North's 1♡ response. North gambled 6◊. West led the ♠10.

Declarer won dummy's ♠A and drew trump. He cashed the ♡A and when East's ♡J fell, he continued the ♡10, hoping that the ♡K and ♡Q would fall together. But West ducked. East won the ♡Q and exited in spades. Eventually, West's ♡K took the setting trick.

Any better attempt to make?

Yes. Try to envision what lie of the cards you need. Hearts is the key. You need to catch two honors doubleton or one honor singleton in either hand. They're almost equally likely, but you have two tie-breakers.

One is the general *Tie-Breaking Principle*: of any two specific layouts of a suit, the more balanced is the more likely. The other is the chance of a defensive slip. A defender with two cards in a suit has a chance to err when the suit is led, but a defender with only one does not. A defender with ♡Kx is unlikely to drop the ♡K under the ♡A if you put him to the test early.

So: ♠A, draw trump, then the ♡A promptly, giving a defender with ♡Kx a chance to play low. Next the ♣A, ♣K, ♠K and ♠Q. Then lead the ♡10, giving West a chance to cover gently with a remaining ♡KJ.

Finally, if you believe in prayer, this is a good time to try it.

DEAL 50. PLAN A AND PLAN B

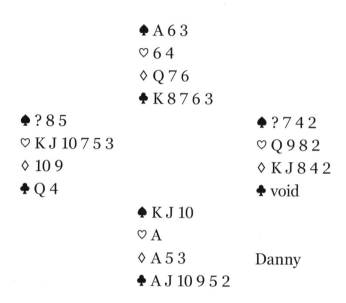

♠ A 6 3
♡ 6 4
◊ Q 7 6
♣ K 8 7 6 3

♠ ? 8 5
♡ K J 10 7 5 3
◊ 10 9
♣ Q 4

♠ ? 7 4 2
♡ Q 9 8 2
◊ K J 8 4 2
♣ void

♠ K J 10
♡ A
◊ A 5 3   Danny
♣ A J 10 9 5 2

West opened a Weak 2♡ Bid on favorable vulnerability. East raised to 3♡ (we'd have bid 4♡). South bid 4♣. North realized that South's 4♣ had come under pressure of preemption and settled for 5♣.

West's ♡J opening lead rode to South's ♡A.

South saw three possible losers: a diamond if the ◊K was with East and a spade if she misguesses the ♠Q. She drew trump, cashed the ◊A just if case the ◊K fell singleton, and led to dummy's ◊Q when it didn't.

East won the ◊K and the ◊J, then exited in hearts. Declarer ruffed.

Danny, who had been kibitzing South, got up to grab a chocolate doughnut before they were all gone. When he returned, South was marking -100 on her scorecard and North and South were quarreling.

North asked him, "Please tell us your Queen-Guessing Rule again. Is it 'Queen on your left' or 'Queen on your right'? I'm not sure I remember."

Danny replied, "Trump queen on your left, other queens on your right. But it's better not to guess. Strip the hearts, then play ace and a low diamond to the queen. If she loses, show your hand and claim. East must either offer a ruff-sluff or break spades for you. Zugzwang!"

DEAL 51. A "PREVENT" OFFENSE

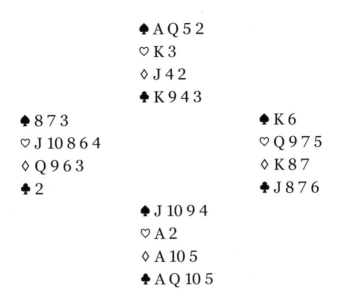

```
              ♠ A Q 5 2
              ♡ K 3
              ◊ J 4 2
              ♣ K 9 4 3
♠ 8 7 3                        ♠ K 6
♡ J 10 8 6 4                   ♡ Q 9 7 5
◊ Q 9 6 3                      ◊ K 8 7
♣ 2                           ♣ J 8 7 6
              ♠ J 10 9 4
              ♡ A 2
              ◊ A 10 5
              ♣ A Q 10 5
```

South opened 1NT and reached 4♠ via Stayman.

West led the ♣ 2. Declarer captured East's ♣J with the ♣A. Suspecting that West's ♣2 was a singleton, he abjured a trump finesse to keep the defenders from scoring a touchdown. He cashed the spade ace and led another to draw trump as quickly as possible.

East won the ♠K and returned the ♣8 for West to ruff with the ♠8. West exited with the ♡J. Declarer had two diamonds to lose. Down one.

A touchdown for the defense! Where did the offense fumble? Could you have held onto the football had you been quarterbacking as South?

Yes, if your vision included the entire field. Clubs wasn't the only problem suit. if you look far enough downfield, you may see the diamonds in the distance, the diamonds on which you played softball before the autumn winds blew chilly and cold.

You must prevent not only the wounding club ruff but also the killing heart exit. So before feeding East the ♠K, cash both top hearts. West will still get his club ruff but now any red-suit exit will be fatal to the defense. You can claim your contract, saying "Ruff-sluff or come to me in diamonds."

DEAL 52. PUSHED AROUND? PUSH BACK!

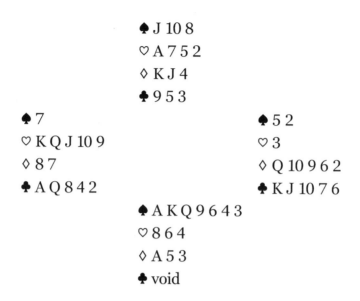

        ♠ J 10 8
        ♡ A 7 5 2
        ◊ K J 4
        ♣ 9 5 3

♠ 7   ♠ 5 2
♡ K Q J 10 9   ♡ 3
◊ 8 7   ◊ Q 10 9 6 2
♣ A Q 8 4 2   ♣ K J 10 7 6

        ♠ A K Q 9 6 4 3
        ♡ 8 6 4
        ◊ A 5 3
        ♣ void

South opened 1♠ and West bid 2♠, Ambiguous Michaels, showing hearts and an unspecified minor. North bid a competitive 3♠. East bid 4NT.

"Blackwood?" asked South.

"No," answered West. "Unusual for the minors."

Not wanting his non-vulnerable opponents to find a profitable save against his vulnerable game, South bid 5♠ and was allowed to play there.

South captured West's ♡K opening lead with the ♡A, drew trump and played on diamonds. When dummy's ◊J lost to East's ◊Q, he remained with two heart losers and went down one.

But a big clue from the bidding made 5♠ a lock. Did you hear it?

West's Michaels Cue Bid marked East with a singleton heart, susceptible to being stripped and thrown in. So, ♡A and ruff a club. Enter dummy twice with trumps to ruff two more clubs. Cash both top diamonds and feed the ◊J to East. With only minor-suit cards left, East must offer a ruff-sluff. Pitch a heart from your hand, ruff with dummy's last trump, lose your last heart and claim 5♠.

DEAL 53. SORRY, WRONG EXIT

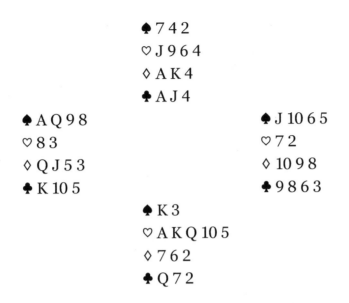

```
              ♠ 7 4 2
              ♡ J 9 6 4
              ◊ A K 4
              ♣ A J 4
♠ A Q 9 8                      ♠ J 10 6 5
♡ 8 3                          ♡ 7 2
◊ Q J 5 3                      ◊ 10 9 8
♣ K 10 5                       ♣ 9 8 6 3
              ♠ K 3
              ♡ A K Q 10 5
              ◊ 7 6 2
              ♣ Q 7 2
```

South opened 1♡ and reached 4♡ via the "Jordan" convention, a 2NT response that shows a limit raise or better over an intervening takeout double, a useful adjunct to the equally useful treatment of jump raises as weak preempts.

West led the ◊Q to dummy's ◊K, under which East dropped the ◊10. South drew trump and finessed the ♣J successfully. Then he cashed dummy's ◊A and led a third diamond, thinking to throw West in. But East's ◊9 won the trick.

East switched to the ♠J. South covered with the ♠K. South lost two spade tricks and ruffed the third spade, but could not escape a club loser at the end. Down one.

Nice try, but not the best. Can you see anything better?

East was the danger hand. To keep him out, South had to duck West's ◊Q at Trick 1. He can win the next diamond and draw trump. Then finesse dummy's ♣J, cash the ♣A and feed the ♣Q to West's ♣K.

Now West is endplayed and must break spades or offer a ruff-sluff.

DEAL 54. OPEN BOOK

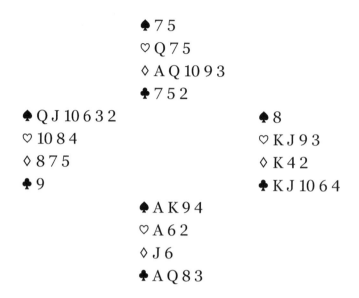

♠ 7 5
♥ Q 7 5
♦ A Q 10 9 3
♣ 7 5 2

♠ Q J 10 6 3 2   ♠ 8
♥ 10 8 4   ♥ K J 9 3
♦ 8 7 5   ♦ K 4 2
♣ 9   ♣ K J 10 6 4

♠ A K 9 4
♥ A 6 2
♦ J 6
♣ A Q 8 3

East opened 1♣. South overcalled 1NT and West bid 2♠. North bid a constructive 3♦ and South bid 3NT. West led the ♠ Queen.

Declarer won the opening lead with the ace and passed the diamond jack. East ducked. Declarer cashed the ♦A and conceded a diamond. East won and returned a club. Declarer won the queen and tried unsuccessfully to reach dummy with the ♥Q. He finished with seven tricks, down two.

Since all the HCP are accounted for, how would you have played?

Since East has the remaining HCP, declarer must try for an endplay. After winning the club finesse, cash the other high spade in case East has another spade to reach this ending.

♠ ---   ♥Q75   ♦109   ♣7

♠--- ♥KJ9 ♦--- ♣K106

♠7 ♥A62 ♦-- - ♣83

Exit with the club eight. East has to win or be endplayed on the next round of clubs. After cashing two rounds of clubs, East has to lead a heart. Declarer has gets two heart tricks and a much needed dummy entry. Nine tricks in all.

DEAL 55. WHEN JIM MET DANNY

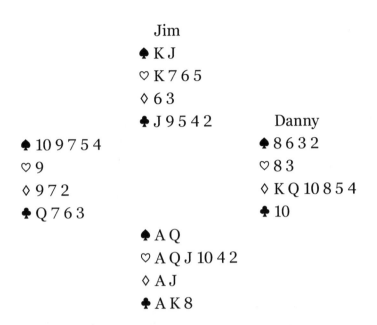

Jim
♠ K J
♡ K 7 6 5
◊ 6 3
♣ J 9 5 4 2

Danny
♠ 8 6 3 2
♡ 8 3
◊ K Q 10 8 5 4
♣ 10

♠ 10 9 7 5 4
♡ 9
◊ 9 7 2
♣ Q 7 6 3

♠ A Q
♡ A Q J 10 4 2
◊ A J
♣ A K 8

South opened an Omnibus 2♣ and North made a neutral 2◊ **response**, leaving room for opener's planned natural rebid. East made a pest of himself with a filthy 3◊ overcall on favorable vulnerability. Danny can be utterly obnoxious when an opponent opens an Omnibus 2♣ against him.

Forced to start strutting her stuff one level higher, South bid 3♡. An ordinary North might have raised to 4♡, but North was Jim. He knew that he'd have had to bid 4♡ with four hearts and a yarborough, so he jumped to 5♡ to show his values. His client bid 6♡ cheerfully.

West led the ◊2 to East's ◊Q and South's ◊A. Declarer drew trump and cashed the ♣AK, hoping the ♣Q would fall. When it didn't, she led her last club to West's ♣Q. When West led the ◊9, South said, "I was hoping your deuce was a singleton," and conceded down one.

"Do you think I'd have bid only three diamonds with eight of them?" asked Danny. "I'd surely have bid five."

"You were in *slam*," said Jim. "Couldn't you try harder?"

"You could have," said Danny. "After I showed out on the second club, take the ace of spades and dummy's king. Lead a diamond though me and your jack will win. You don't think I'd let you endplay me, do you?"

DEAL 56. TAKE ME OUT TO THE BALL GAME

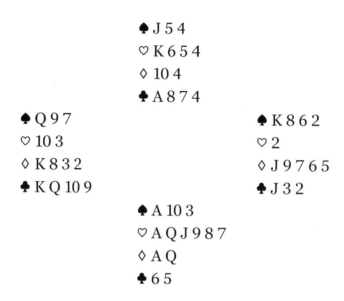

```
                    ♠ J 5 4
                    ♡ K 6 5 4
                    ◊ 10 4
                    ♣ A 8 7 4
    ♠ Q 9 7                         ♠ K 8 6 2
    ♡ 10 3                          ♡ 2
    ◊ K 8 3 2                       ◊ J 9 7 6 5
    ♣ K Q 10 9                      ♣ J 3 2
                    ♠ A 10 3
                    ♡ A Q J 9 8 7
                    ◊ A Q
                    ♣ 6 5
```

West led the ♣K against 4♡ reached via a 1♡ opening and 2♡ raise.

Declarer won dummy's ♣A (Strike 1) and the ♡AK. He finessed the ◊Q (Strike 2). West won the ◊K and continued clubs. South ruffed the third club and unblocked the ◊A but then he had to tackle spades himself.

With the missing honors split, South had to lose a second spade trick. Strike 3, you're out!

Good pitching, or swinging at pitches outside the strike zone?

Shoulda brought in Eddie Stanky to pinch hit!

Of your four losers, you can only avoid a second spade loser for sure ... by a strip and throw-in. For this you need two timely dummy entries. The ♣A is one, but you must wait to use it until you're ready to ruff clubs.

So duck the ♣K (Ball 1). Suppose West shifts to ♡3. Win the ♡9 and ♡A. Take the ♣A and ruff a club (Ball 2). Cross to the ♡K and ruff dummy's last club (Ball 3). Cash the ◊A and exit with the ◊Q (Ball 4).

Whoever wins the ◊K must offer a ruff-sluff or break spades. Here West will win. Walk to first base and claim your contract.

DEAL 57. DÉJÀ VU ALL OVER AGAIN?

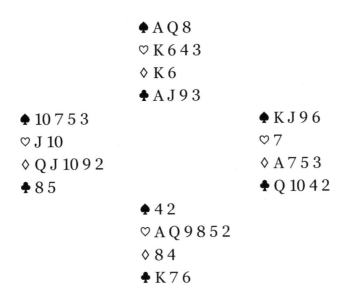

```
                    ♠ A Q 8
                    ♡ K 6 4 3
                    ◇ K 6
                    ♣ A J 9 3
   ♠ 10 7 5 3                      ♠ K J 9 6
   ♡ J 10                          ♡ 7
   ◇ Q J 10 9 2                    ◇ A 7 5 3
   ♣ 8 5                           ♣ Q 10 4 2
                    ♠ 4 2
                    ♡ A Q 9 8 5 2
                    ◇ 8 4
                    ♣ K 7 6
```

When Danny was young, he had a superb memory. In a Manhattan tournament, he picked up a hand and thought "Déjà vu!" He called for a director. The legendary director Harry Goldwater arrived. Danny left the table and whispered to him, "I saw this deal in Cleveland seven years ago."

Harry asked Danny to describe his partner's hand. Danny called it off card-for-card. "I won't say if you're right," said Harry. "But if your memory is that good, you're entitled to take advantage." Whereupon Danny reached 3NT and made five. All his counterparts stopped in 1NT and made three.

Sixty years later, Danny held the North hand at a club in West Los Angeles. When South opened a Weak 2♡, it was déjà vu all over again. He called a director and whispered, "I played this deal two weeks ago Friday." He recited the South hand omitting only the spot cards. The director told him to play the deal as though he hadn't seen it.

Danny remembered that three finesses worked, but conscience led him to bid the normal 4♡, against which West led the ◇Q.

Strange. Two weeks prior, *East* had held ◇QJ10xx. Now three losing finesses later, Danny's client was down one, but was there any way home?

Yes. Duck the ◇Q, as East is marked with the ◇A. After a second diamond, an eventual first-round club finesse endplays East. A club shift lets you win in hand and later feed East his ◇A to endplay him. Even on a spade shift, you can win the ♠A, draw trump and throw East in with the ◇A.

DEAL 58. WRONG DUMMY? LISTEN

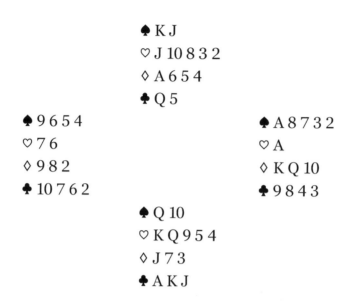

```
              ♠ K J
              ♡ J 10 8 3 2
              ◊ A 6 5 4
              ♣ Q 5
♠ 9 6 5 4                    ♠ A 8 7 3 2
♡ 7 6                        ♡ A
◊ 9 8 2                      ◊ K Q 10
♣ 10 7 6 2                   ♣ 9 8 4 3
              ♠ Q 10
              ♡ K Q 9 5 4
              ◊ J 7 3
              ♣ A K J
```

East opened 1♠ in second seat and South overcalled 2♡. North's 2♠ cue bid showed a stronger heart raise than a simple 3♡ and South accepted the implied invitation to 4♡.

West led the ♠ 4.

East took the first two tricks with his aces and exited safely in spades. South perused the dummy. Not what he hoped for: two spades opposite two, a self-duplicating doubleton ♣Q, and neither second- nor third-round diamond control.

South saw only one glimmer of hope: a doubleton ◊K or ◊Q in either defender's hand. He drew the last trump, led to dummy's ◊A and led another diamond. East took the ◊Q and ◊K. Down one.

Was there a second glimmer that declarer overlooked?

Yes. East's second-seat opening virtually marked him with all the missing high cards. Including the ◊K and ◊Q. So after drawing the last trump, cash both top clubs, ruff the useless ♣J in dummy, lead a low diamond from dummy, and watch East sweat futilely after winning the ◊Q or ◊K. It's either a ruff-sluff or a lead from the remaining diamond monarch.

DEAL 59. BACKFIRE

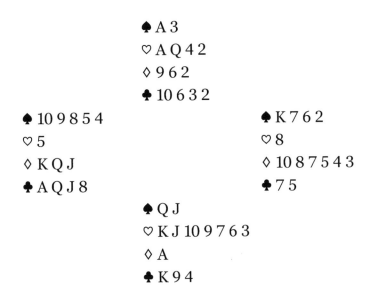

```
                    ♠ A 3
                    ♡ A Q 4 2
                    ◊ 9 6 2
                    ♣ 10 6 3 2
♠ 10 9 8 5 4                    ♠ K 7 6 2
♡ 5                            ♡ 8
◊ K Q J                        ◊ 10 8 7 5 4 3
♣ A Q J 8                      ♣ 7 5
                    ♠ Q J
                    ♡ K J 10 9 7 6 3
                    ◊ A
                    ♣ K 9 4
```

South opened 1♡ on favorable vulnerability. Though some might have doubled with his hand, West overcalled 1♠. North bid 4♡, not being sure he wanted to sell out to 3♠ if he were to give East room to bid it.

West made the obvious ◊K opening lead. Declarer won perforce and drew trump with the ♡K. He then took the "obvious" spade finesse, falling off his chair when East produced the ♠K and returned the ♣7 promptly.

Two strong kibitzers watching the nickel game in the corner rushed over to pick declarer up, but when the smoke cleared, he eventually lost three club tricks. Down one.

"How could you overcall on that suit?" cried South.

"Why not," said North. "They make four spades. I'd never find the defense of giving you a diamond ruff. But you could claim four hearts if you'd troubled to figure out the sure way to make it. This isn't a duplicate club where they pay extra for overtricks."

Was North right? How should you play to lock up your contract?

Yes. Lead the ♡J to dummy's ♡A at Trick 2. Ruff a diamond high. Lead the ♡10 to dummy's ♡Q and ruff the last diamond high. Lead the ♠Q and play dummy's ♠A even if West doesn't cover. Lead dummy's ♠3. If East wins and shifts to clubs, cover a quack or duck a spot-card and claim 4♡.

DEAL 60. SEVEN IS THE PIP

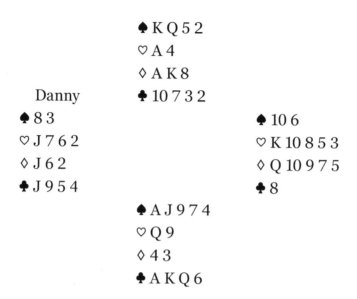

♠ K Q 5 2
♡ A 4
◇ A K 8
♣ 10 7 3 2

Danny
♠ 8 3
♡ J 7 6 2
◇ J 6 2
♣ J 9 5 4

♠ 10 6
♡ K 10 8 5 3
◇ Q 10 9 7 5
♣ 8

♠ A J 9 7 4
♡ Q 9
◇ 4 3
♣ A K Q 6

With both sides vul on the last deal of the chukker, South opened 1♠.

In their methods, North's 2NT response to South's 1♠ opening was a Jacoby Forcing Raise, denying shortness. South's 3NT rebid, per system, also denied shortness and showed a good 15 to bad 18 points. North bid 6♠ without further ado.

With little to go on, West guessed to lead the ♡2.

"Danny's a notorious king-underleader," said South. "If he's done it again this time, I can make seven."

He looked at the score and said, "The rubber's even. Seven is the pip!" as he pulled the ♡4 from dummy.

"I'd settle for six," said North, who was already -37 on the backscore.

"I'll settle for down two," said East as he won the ♡K and led the ♣8. We needn't narrate the rest of the play. Down one, losing a club at the end

"Couldn't be helped," said South. But could it?

Yes. Unless trumps split 4-0, 6♠ is a lock. Rise with the ♡A and draw trump. Cash the ◇AK and ruff a diamond. Cash the ♣AK and if clubs split badly, feed the ♡Q to whichever defender has the ♡K. He'll have to give you a ruff-sluff or the rest of your clubs.

DEAL 61. NO WAY OUT

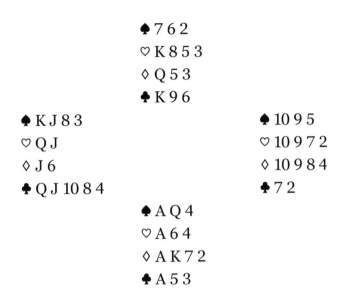

```
              ♠ 7 6 2
              ♡ K 8 5 3
              ◇ Q 5 3
              ♣ K 9 6
♠ K J 8 3                      ♠ 10 9 5
♡ Q J                          ♡ 10 9 7 2
◇ J 6                          ◇ 10 9 8 4
♣ Q J 10 8 4                   ♣ 7 2
              ♠ A Q 4
              ♡ A 6 4
              ◇ A K 7 2
              ♣ A 5 3
```

With flat shape, North eschewed Stayman and raised South's 2NT opening directly to 3NT. West led the ♣Q.

Declarer counted eight tricks and saw many chances for ninth: hearts 3-3, diamonds 3-3, or a spade finesse as a last resort.

South ducked the ♣Q and won the ♣10 continuation in hand. He ducked a heart and won West's ♣J with the ♣K. Then he tried the top hearts and top diamonds. When neither red suit split 3-3, he tried the spade finesse. Not today. He lost three clubs, a heart, and a spade. Down one.

Unlucky or poor technique?

Declarer erred at Trick 1 when he gave up his *feeders* prematurely. Proper technique is to win the first club with the ♣K, duck a heart, and win the next club with the ♣A. Then cash both top hearts. On discovering the

4-2 heart split, cash three top diamonds.

When diamonds split 4-2 also, it's time to stuff West in with the ♣9 feeder. West can cash two more clubs, but then he, not you, must break spades, leading up to your waiting ♠AQ.

DEAL 62. 75% OR 100%?

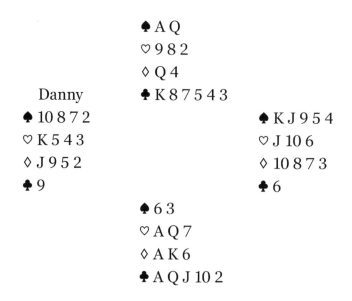

```
                    ♠ A Q
                    ♡ 9 8 2
                    ◊ Q 4
      Danny         ♣ K 8 7 5 4 3
      ♠ 10 8 7 2                    ♠ K J 9 5 4
      ♡ K 5 4 3                     ♡ J 10 6
      ◊ J 9 5 2                     ◊ 10 8 7 3
      ♣ 9                           ♣ 6
                    ♠ 6 3
                    ♡ A Q 7
                    ◊ A K 6
                    ♣ A Q J 10 2
```

South opened 2NT. North bid 3NT which they played as a transfer to clubs. South bid 4◊, a Roman Keycard Super-Accept showing three keys. North's 4♡ next was the Queen Ask, and South's 5◊ reply showed the ♣Q and the ◊K. North's 5NT was a retransfer to 6♣, which North passed.

"That'll be 25 cents each," said Danny, West, as he led the ♣2. "I own the patent on Roman Key-Card Super-Accepts."

South, the Secretary-Treasurer of the Los Angeles Finesse Society, flipped two quarters on the table for the partnership. He saw two finesses. If either was successful, the slam bonus would more than cover the 50-cent investment. First he tried the ♠Q, which lost to East's ♠K. When the heart finesse lost also, he was down one with no return for his 50 cents.

South bewailed the failure of a 75% chance, but North insisted it was 100%. Who was right?

North. Spot cards mean a lot. The ♡9, ♡8 *and* ♡7 made 6♣ cold. Win the ♠A, draw trump, take three top diamonds to discard dummy's ♠Q and ruff the ♠6 to strip the suit. Lead any heart from dummy and cover any heart East plays. After West wins, he is endplayed.

Danny is still working on a slam convention to locate the seven of any given side suit. Anyone want to invest in his project?

DEAL 63. NO FINESSES, PLEASE

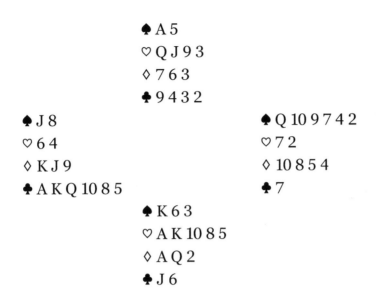

```
                    ♠ A 5
                    ♡ Q J 9 3
                    ◊ 7 6 3
                    ♣ 9 4 3 2
   ♠ J 8                              ♠ Q 10 9 7 4 2
   ♡ 6 4                              ♡ 7 2
   ◊ K J 9                            ◊ 10 8 5 4
   ♣ A K Q 10 8 5                     ♣ 7
                    ♠ K 6 3
                    ♡ A K 10 8 5
                    ◊ A Q 2
                    ♣ J 6
```

South opened 1♡. West overcalled 2♣. North raised to 2♡ and East risked 2♠ on favorable vulnerability, a bit pushy to be sure, but not forcing in his or most pairs' methods. South upgraded his ♠K and bid 4♡.

West led and continued high clubs. Declarer ruffed the third and drew trump with the ♡A and ♡J. Then he finessed the ◊Q. West won the ◊K and tapped South with the ♣10.

With no place to park his remaining diamond loser, South went down one.

But do you see how to lock up the contract after finding trumps 2-2?

Cash the ♠A and ♠K, then ruff your last spade in dummy. Now feed dummy's ♣9 to West's ♣10 while discarding the ◊2. As both black suits have been stripped, West is endplayed and must offer a ruff-sluff or a free diamond finesse.

DEAL 64. HOPING FOR THE BEST

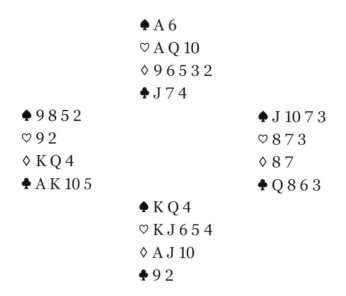

♠ A 6
♡ A Q 10
◊ 9 6 5 3 2
♣ J 7 4

♠ 9 8 5 2
♡ 9 2
◊ K Q 4
♣ A K 10 5

♠ J 10 7 3
♡ 8 7 3
◊ 8 7
♣ Q 8 6 3

♠ K Q 4
♡ K J 6 5 4
◊ A J 10
♣ 9 2

South opened 1♡ and West made a take-out double. Lacking the fourth heart needed for a "Jordan" 2NT, North redoubled to show a stronger-than-average hand and create a forcing auction.

As a prophylactic against West's possible self-rescue to 2◊, East bid 1♠, showing at least four spades and at least one card higher than a 4-spot.

When 1♠ rolled round to North, he bid 2♡ to show a "three-card limit raise."

This slow auction permitted the pair to slide into 3NT via a 2NT game try but instead South crawled up to 3♡ and North bid a precarious 4♡.

Playing Patriarch Opening Leads, West led the ♣A, showing the ♣K while denying the ♣Q. East encouraged, so West continued the ♣K and ♣5.

South ruffed, drew trump, and oblivious to the bidding, finessed diamonds twice. Down one.

But you heard the bidding; how would you try to make 4♡?

As dummy has only three trumps, try for an endplay with a partial elimination. As West doubled hearts for takeout he figures to have no more than two. Strip the spades and draw only two rounds of trump ending in dummy. Deep-finesse in diamonds, expecting West to win. When he does he's endplayed, forced to give you a free finesse in diamonds or a ruff-sluff.

DEAL 65. NOT PERFECT, BUT GIVE IT A TRY

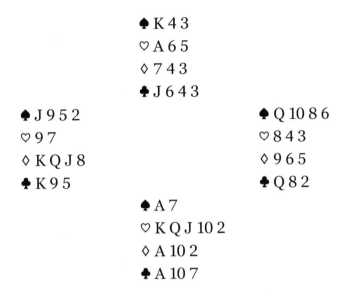

♠ K 4 3
♡ A 6 5
◇ 7 4 3
♣ J 6 4 3

♠ J 9 5 2
♡ 9 7
◇ K Q J 8
♣ K 9 5

♠ Q 10 8 6
♡ 8 4 3
◇ 9 6 5
♣ Q 8 2

♠ A 7
♡ K Q J 10 2
◇ A 10 2
♣ A 10 7

We can hardly blame South for bidding 4♡ after North raised his 1♡ opening to 2♡, especially at rubber bridge where there are still bonuses for 100 and 150 honors. But as often happens when one partner has a pancake and the other has a waffle (Danny's terms for 4-3-3-3 and 5-3-3-2 hands), 3NT is a lock and four of a major is iffy.

West led the ◇K and declarer could see only the same eight tricks he'd have in notrump. Lack of a fourth trump in dummy precluded a full strip and throw-in.

So declarer won the ◇A, drew trump ending in dummy, and worked on clubs. When he led the ♣3 to his ♣10, West won the ♣K and took the next two tricks with diamonds. South ruffed the fourth diamond, but when the ♣Q didn't fall under his ♣A, he had to lose another club to East's ♣Q.

Down one. How would you play the club suit to avoid two losers?

We hope you answered, "I didn't, they did." When a full elimination is impossible, try a partial elimination. Duck the first diamond, win next and draw only two rounds of trump. Cash both top spades and ruff a spade.

Now lead the ◇10. You'll hit the jackpot, specifically West's ◇J. If he doesn't have the last trump, he'll either break clubs for you, holding your club losers to one, or give you a ruff-sluff.

CHAPTER TWO

TRUMP
ENDPLAYS

In this chapter we focus more on the trump suit. What makes endplays more frequent in suit play is the threat of a ruff-sluff.

Often the exit card is a trump card (Big hint).

DEAL 66. CAKE FOR DESSERT

♠ K 10 9 3
♡ Q 2
◊ 10 7 4
♣ K 8 5 3

South	West	North	East
1♠	2◊	2♠	pass
3♣	pass	4♠	(All pass)

♠ A J 8 6 2
♡ A K 5
◊ J 3
♣ A 7 2

Opening Lead: ◊K

West continued with the ◊A and ◊Q. Declarer ruffed and tried to guess how to play trumps: Finesse East for the ♠Q, on the Theory of Open Spaces (West has eight non-diamonds, East has ten) or heed Mother Goose ("Eight ever, nine never!")?

We won't tell you how the actual South guessed, except to tell you that in this book guessers always guess wrong. Any way to have your cake and eat it too?

Yes. If you can strip West of safe exit cards, you can afford to lose a trick to his doubleton or tripleton ♠Q.

After ruffing the third diamond, cash the ♣A and lead the ♣7. If West shows out and ruffs, he ruffs air and your club loser goes away. Otherwise, you'll win dummy's ♣K, cash the ♡Q and take two more hearts, In the unlikely event that West ruffs the third heart, you'll overruff in dummy and avoid a trump loser.

Now with both red suits stripped, you can lead low to dummy's ♠K and continue with dummy's ♠10. If East shows out, you'll win the ♠A and throw West in with his ♠Q. If East follows low, you'll finesse.

West may win the ♠Q, but unless he has a third club, he'll have to give you a ruff-sluff and surrender the rest.

No guarantees, but a very good bet. If West does not have the ♠Q, you'll eat your cake. But most of the time that he does, you'll have it too.

DEAL 67. WHICH OF THREE FINESSES?

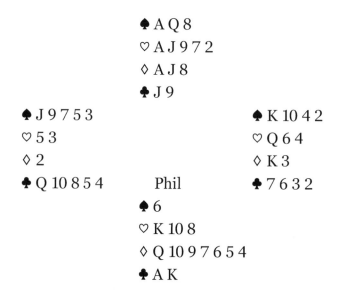

```
                    ♠ A Q 8
                    ♡ A J 9 7 2
                    ◊ A J 8
                    ♣ J 9
♠ J 9 7 5 3                         ♠ K 10 4 2
♡ 5 3                              ♡ Q 6 4
◊ 2                                ◊ K 3
♣ Q 10 8 5 4        Phil           ♣ 7 6 3 2
                    ♠ 6
                    ♡ K 10 8
                    ◊ Q 10 9 7 6 5 4
                    ♣ A K
```

South opened 1◊ and rebid 2◊ over North's 1♡ response, suppressing good three-card heart support temporarily. North rebid 3♣, to create a game force. Having limited his hand with 2◊, South jumped to 4♡, whereupon North gambled 6◊.

West, viewing North's 3♣ rebid suspiciously, led the ♣5.

South, Phil Finessoholic, tried a trump finesse first. East won and exited in trump. Then Phil cashed the ♡A and ♡K, trying to drop a short ♡Q. We're proud of you, Phil! Just last year, you'd have tried to guess the ♡Q. This way, he had another chance; if the ♡Q didn't fall, he could fall back on the spade finesse as a last resort. Alas, when he did, that finesse lost too. Down two, minus 100.

It was a team game, and his team lost two IMPs, as 6◊ went down only one in the other room. Some days it doesn't pay to get out of bed.

But was there a better line of play?

How about no finesses and no guesses? Instead, try a strip and throw-in. ♣A, ♠A, spade ruff. Lead the ◊Q hoping West covers, and play dummy's ◊A when he doesn't. Ruff dummy's ♠Q and cash the ♣K. Now feed a trump trick to the defender who has the ◊K. He's endplayed.

He must give you a ruff-sluff or guess hearts for you. You'll *make* 6◊.

DEAL 68. IMPLIED COUNT

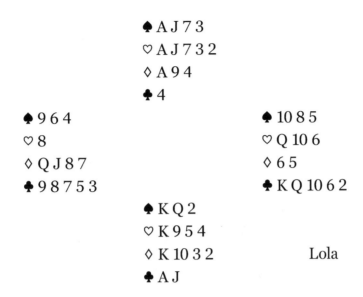

♠ A J 7 3
♥ A J 7 3 2
♦ A 9 4
♣ 4

♠ 9 6 4
♥ 8
♦ Q J 8 7
♣ 9 8 7 5 3

♠ 10 8 5
♥ Q 10 6
♦ 6 5
♣ K Q 10 6 2

♠ K Q 2
♥ K 9 5 4
♦ K 10 3 2
♣ A J

Lola

South opened 1NT. East doubled North's "Stayman" 2♣ response for the lead, When South bid 2♥, in their methods denying four spades, North had visions of slam. He invoked OMAR, "Other Major Relays," bidding 2♠ to ask for shape. South replied 2NT, denying a five-card suit anywhere. North's 4♣ next was a splinter slam try, showing a singleton (4♣ directly over 2♥ would have shown a void). With only the ♣J wasted, South liked his hand for slam. He used a "Kickback" 4♠ to ask for keys, and then bid 6♥ over North's three-key 4NT reply. *Don't try this at home!*

West led the ♣9.

Declarer won Tricks 1, 2 and 3 with the ♣A, ♥K and ♥A. Oops, a trump loser, grim prospects. He turned to Lola, his right-hand kibitzer, and said, "Aren't your friends Jim and Danny writing a book on endplays?"

Lola only smiled. South smiled too as he ran spades. On the fourth spade East ruffed with the ♥Q. South exclaimed "Endplayed!" as East led the ♦6. South played for split honors, but West had them both. Down one.

Could you have survived the bad breaks?

We hope so. Before leading the last spade, take the ♦K and ♦A and ruff the ♣J in dummy. Then, whether East ruffs the ♠J with his ♥Q or waits to be thrown in with it next, he's endplayed. A ruff-sluff, and 6♥ makes!

DEAL 69. NO ESCAPE

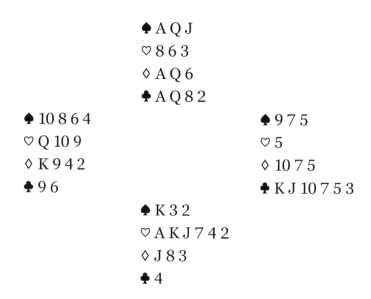

East opened 3♣ on favorable vulnerability, South overcalled 3♡, a bit light. North bid 6♡, a reasonable gamble. West led the ♣9.

Declarer rose with dummy's ♣A and cashed the ♡AK. He finessed the ◊Q successfully and cashed three spades. He threw West in with the ♡Q, but West had safe exits in both black suits. South ruffed West's club exit and could not avoid losing a diamond at the end. Down one.

South started on the right trail but got sidetracked. Could you have made it to the finish line?

Not an easy deal. Unlucky to have a trump loser, but South can recover. After getting the bad news, lead a spade to dummy and ruff a club, West follows; lucky you, for if he is out of clubs he can ruff and exit in spades to beat you. Cash two more spades and ruff another club. West will do well to discard a diamond, for if he overruffs he'll be endplayed.

But that just prolongs the inevitable. Finesse the ◊Q. When it holds, you can ruff dummy's last club. Again West must discard. This time he must throw a spade to avoid blanking the ◊K.

Finally, you can feed your ♡J to his ♡Q. In the two-card ending he must lead from his remaining ◊Kx through dummy's ◊A6 up to your ◊J8. No escape for poor West! 6♡ makes.

DEAL 70. DO THE BEST YOU CAN

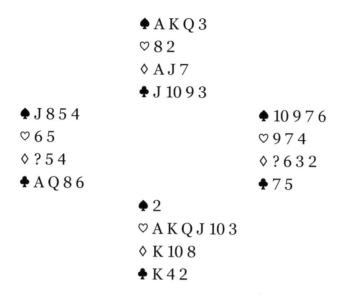

♠ A K Q 3
♡ 8 2
◇ A J 7
♣ J 10 9 3

♠ J 8 5 4
♡ 6 5
◇ ? 5 4
♣ A Q 8 6

♠ 10 9 7 6
♡ 9 7 4
◇ ? 6 3 2
♣ 7 5

♠ 2
♡ A K Q J 10 3
◇ K 10 8
♣ K 4 2

South opened 1♡ and jumped to 3♡ over North's 1♠ response. North bid 4◇, often a second suit. When South bid 4♡, North's 5♡ raise revealed that he had the ◇A for his 4◇ bid and was worried about the unbid suit, clubs. for slam. Having second-round club control, North bid 6♡.

West led a passive ♡6 against 6♡. Declarer finished trumps and threw low clubs on dummy's spades. Then he led to his ♣K. West won and exited with his last spade. Declarer ruffed and tried to guess the ◇Q.

You know how the story ends in this book. Finesses and guesses alike fail. Down one. Could you have eliminated the need to guess?

Maybe. You could have increased your chances by ruffing dummy's last spade to remove a safe exit card when spades split 4-4.

As it happens, West will win the ♣A and will be endplayed, A diamond shift guesses the ◇Q for you. A club return lets you discard a diamond on one of dummy's clubs,

No guarantees that this will work. On some other layout, East may have the ♣A and put you to a guess with a low club return. Would he do so if he also had the ♣Q? We don't think so. But if worst comes to worst and nothing else works, you can try to guess the ◇Q.

DEAL 71. "NINE NEVER," "OPEN SPACES," OR WHAT?

♠ 8 3 2
♡ K 9 8 6
♢ A 8 2
♣ A K 7

♠ Q 4
♡ A J 10 3 2
♢ K J 6 5
♣ 8 6

North bid 1♣ and raised South's 1♡ response to 2♡. South bid 4♡.

West led the ♠7. East won the ♠A and returned the ♠10. West won the ♠K and continued the ♠J. East discarded the ♣5 and South ruffed.

Both defenders followed low when South led to dummy's ♡K. Now he was on the horns of a dilemma: where is the missing ♡Q?

Horn Number 1: Mother Goose says. "Eight ever. nine never!"

Horn Number 2: the Theory of Open Spaces says that West has 7 known cards (6 spades and 1 heart) but East has 4 known cards (2 spades and a presumed 2 low hearts, so it's 9 to 6 that East has the ♡Q.

Horns Number 3 and 4: West had ♠KJ9765 but didn't bid spades: was it because he was too weak (no ♡Q) or because he was too balanced (no singleton)? What is a dilemma doing with two extra horns anyway?

We won't tell you who had the ♡Q, but if you guessed that West had the ♢Q, you guessed right. The actual declarer guessed wrong. Down one.

Could you steer more safely among all four horns of this dilemma?

Yes, with a strip-and-endplay. Cash the ♡K and ♣AK. Ruff the ♣7 with the ♡J. Now lead to the ♢A and let dummy's ♡9 ride if not covered. Even if West wins a doubleton ♡Q, he'll be endplayed. Either a diamond into your ♢KJ or a ruff-sluff in a black suit assures the contract.

DEAL 72. WORTH A TRY

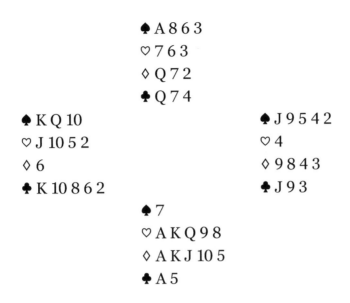

♠ A 8 6 3
♡ 7 6 3
◊ Q 7 2
♣ Q 7 4

♠ K Q 10
♡ J 10 5 2
◊ 6
♣ K 10 8 6 2

♠ J 9 5 4 2
♡ 4
◊ 9 8 4 3
♣ J 9 3

♠ 7
♡ A K Q 9 8
◊ A K J 10 5
♣ A 5

South opened a strong artificial 2♣ and rebid 2♡ over North's neutral 2◊ response. They were using the wonderful Eric Kokish's brainchild "Birthright" in which 2♡ served double-duty to show either hearts or a game-forcing balanced hand. North bid the required 2♠ for clarification and took a 3♡ preference when South bid 3◊ to shown hearts and diamonds.

Several cue bids later, they reached 6♡.

West led the ♠K to dummy's ♠A. Declarer drew the ♡A, the ♡K and … oops, East showed out. Wriggle and squirm as he tried, declarer could not avoid losing a trump and a club. Down one.

Could you do better than wriggle and squirm?

As often happens, the answer is "Maybe." It can't hurt to try. So while hoping for the best (three-two hearts or West having a singleton honor), prepare for the second best: a defender with a trump trick having to lead from the ♣K after winning his trump trick. To cater to this unlikely but still possible circumstance, try to make life difficult for a defender with a trump trick by stripping him of diamond and spade out-cards.

Use your Trick 1 dummy entry to ruff a spade. Then cash three top trumps. When you see the bad split, cross to dummy's ◊Q to ruff another spade. West's last spade falls. Lead diamonds until he ruffs in and … it's "Come to papa in clubs!" 6♡ makes.

DEAL 73. GOOD NEWS, BAD NEWS

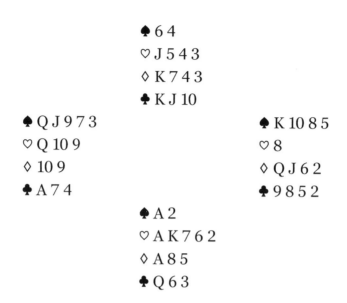

```
                    ♠ 6 4
                    ♡ J 5 4 3
                    ◊ K 7 4 3
                    ♣ K J 10
♠ Q J 9 7 3                          ♠ K 10 8 5
♡ Q 10 9                             ♡ 8
◊ 10 9                              ◊ Q J 6 2
♣ A 7 4                             ♣ 9 8 5 2
                    ♠ A 2
                    ♡ A K 7 6 2
                    ◊ A 8 5
                    ♣ Q 6 3
```

In this era of fancy bidding, it was refreshing to see a perfectly adequate 1♡-2♡-3♡-4♡ auction.

South won West's ♠Q opening lead with the ♠A and cashed both top hearts. When the ♡Q didn't fall, declarer faced a loser in each suit. No way home from here! Down one.

Could you have given 4♡ a better shot?

Yes, if you'd stopped to ask yourself, "What might go wrong?"

Nothing, if the ♡Q falls in the first two rounds of trump. So assume that a defender has three hearts to the queen and play accordingly. Your only hope then is for a defender to have no safe exit when he wins the ♡Q.

The only suit in which you might avoid a loser is diamonds. That's the suit you must eliminate last. Duck West's ♠Q to get the elimination started. Win the next spade, or a diamond shift, and cash the ♡A. When the ♡Q doesn't fall, retain the ♡K and attack clubs to drive out the ♣A. Only when it is gone should you take the ♡K and any uncashed diamond and club tricks.

Finally, feed a heart to West's ♡Q and pray that her jewelry case is empty of diamonds. You're in luck! The Great Jeweler in the Sky heeds your prayer. West has only spades left, so she must give you a ruff-sluff and your contract on a silver platter. Making 4♡.

DEAL 74. THE EASY WAY

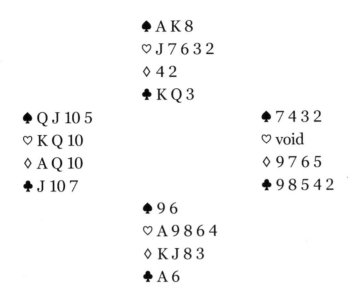

♠ A K 8
♡ J 7 6 3 2
♢ 4 2
♣ K Q 3

♠ Q J 10 5   ♠ 7 4 3 2
♡ K Q 10   ♡ void
♢ A Q 10   ♢ 9 7 6 5
♣ J 10 7   ♣ 9 8 5 4 2

♠ 9 6
♡ A 9 8 6 4
♢ K J 8 3
♣ A 6

South opened 1♡ on Deal 4 of the chukker. West, a stubborn old curmudgeon, might have opened 1NT had he dealt, but he refuses to play 1NT overcalls as natural, so he passed. North's 2NT response wasn't natural, it was an artificial forcing raise, of which many versions have proliferated over the last few decades. His was a Jacoby Forcing Raise, the most popular, which required opener to show shortness or extra strength, or jump to 4♡ with neither (a treatment called "Fast Arrival Shows Trash").

West led the ♠Q against 4♡. South won dummy's ♠K. A heart to the ♡A brought the bad news. Declarer returned to dummy with the ♠A to lead the ♢2. East played the ♢7 and South started to mumble, "Eeny, meany, ..." but before he got to "mo" West showed his hand and claimed: "I'll take two diamonds and two hearts. Down one, 100 for us above the line, and let's settle up. I have an early dinner date and want to get out of here."

Unlucky, or tired at the end of a long afternoon of three-cent bridge?

Maybe both. South should have done his thinking before touching diamonds. This deal is a simple example of a trump endplay. Upon getting the bad news in trump, strip both black suits by ruffing a spade and cashing the clubs to pitch a diamond. Then throw West in with a trump. He can cash another trump but must then lead diamonds or give a ruff-sluff.

No "Eeny, meany, miney, mo" and West still gets to leave early.

DEAL 75. YOUR LEAD

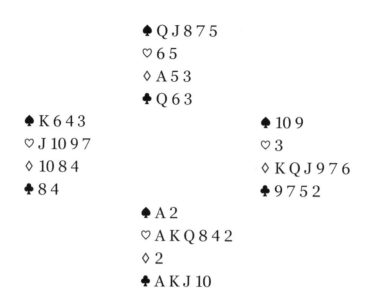

```
                    ♠ Q J 8 7 5
                    ♡ 6 5
                    ♢ A 5 3
                    ♣ Q 6 3
♠ K 6 4 3                           ♠ 10 9
♡ J 10 9 7                          ♡ 3
♢ 10 8 4                            ♢ K Q J 9 7 6
♣ 8 4                              ♣ 9 7 5 2
                    ♠ A 2
                    ♡ A K Q 8 4 2
                    ♢ 2
                    ♣ A K J 10
```

East opened a Weak 2♢ Bid on favorable vulnerability. Weak 2♢ Bids don't shut out 2♡ or 2♠ overcalls, but this one shut out South's intended powerhouse 2♣ opening. South made a slightly off-shape takeout double, almost certain that North would reply in spades, but when North jumped to 3♠, he was happy to gamble 6♡.

"I hope the king of spades is off," said South as West's ♢4 opening lead hit the table. "Else we may have missed seven."

North quaked and hoped silently, "Please just try to make six!"

South won dummy's ♢A and cashed two top hearts. When East showed out on the second, he thought briefly of declaring an unfairity but held his tongue. He crossed to dummy's ♣Q to let the ♠Q ride. You know what happens to finesses in this book. Down one, as West won the ♠K and waited for his trump trick.

"Why don't my 50-50 finesses ever work?" griped South.

"I make it 50-20 against," said North. Could you buck such odds?

Yes, if you strip the minors. Start by ruffing a diamond at Trick 2. Cash the ♡AKQ. Cross to the ♣Q and ruff another diamond. Now run clubs. Whether West ruffs in or waits for you to throw him in with the last trump, he must lead spades to you. Making 6♡. Well bid, gentlemen!

DEAL 76. DON'T TOUCH THEM

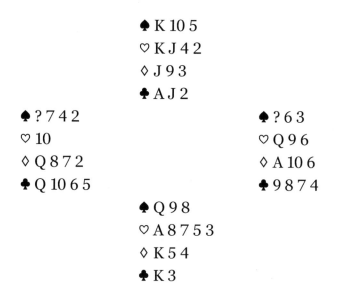

♠ K 10 5
♡ K J 4 2
◊ J 9 3
♣ A J 2

♠ ? 7 4 2
♡ 10
◊ Q 8 7 2
♣ Q 10 6 5

♠ ? 6 3
♡ Q 9 6
◊ A 10 6
♣ 9 8 7 4

♠ Q 9 8
♡ A 8 7 5 3
◊ K 5 4
♣ K 3

South responded 1♡ to North's 1♣ and bid 4♡ over North's 2♡ raise.

West led the ◊2. East won the ◊A and returned the ◊10 to South's ◊K.

South cashed the ♡A and led to dummy's ♡A, learning the bad news. With a heart, a diamond and at least one spade still to lose, it was "Last Resort" time for declarer. He led to his ♣K and finessed dummy's ♣J. Don't say finesses *never* work in this book. When it's necessary to take them, they do. He threw his last diamond on dummy's ♣A.

Finally, he attacked spades. Danny has a queen-guessing rule but no jack-guessing rule, so we have no advice there. South misguessed and lost two spade tricks. Down one.

How would you play the spades?

We hope you answered, "I wouldn't touch them." After discarding a diamond on the ♣A, ruff dummy's last diamond, setting the stage. Then feed a trump to East's ♡Q. Now East will be endplayed and break spades for you. You'll lose one spade trick and make 4♡.

DEAL 77. NOTHING TO LOSE

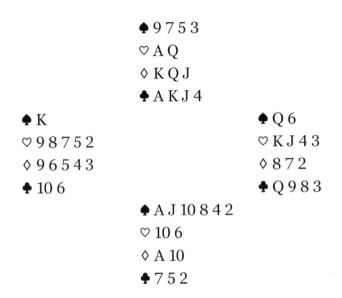

```
                    ♠ 9 7 5 3
                    ♡ A Q
                    ◊ K Q J
                    ♣ A K J 4
♠ K                                    ♠ Q 6
♡ 9 8 7 5 2                            ♡ K J 4 3
◊ 9 6 5 4 3                            ◊ 8 7 2
♣ 10 6                                 ♣ Q 9 8 3
                    ♠ A J 10 8 4 2
                    ♡ 10 6
                    ◊ A 10
                    ♣ 7 5 2
```

South opened a Weak 2♠ Bid on adverse vulnerability. North bid a Roman Keycard Blackwood 4NT, and on learning from South's 5♡ reply that only one key and the ♠Q were missing, gambled 6♠, As little as ♠AKxxxx ♡xx ◊xxx ♣Qx opposite would make slam a big favorite.

West led the ♡9.

Thinking that West would not be leading the ♡9 from a holding that included the ♡K, South rose with the ♡A. He cashed three diamonds to discard the ♡10. Then he cashed the ♣A and crossed to the ♠A.

When he finessed the ♣J next, East won both black queens.

South went down one. Did he suffer from a blind spot?

Yes. Had he ruffed dummy's last heart promptly before cashing the black aces, he'd have better than a 50-50 chance of avoiding the club finesse. Then South can feed a trump to the defender with the ♠Q.

If East has the ♠Q, he's endplayed. If West has the ♠Q. he might not have another club for safe exit. But if he does, a club finesse remains as a last resort. Nothing to lose!

DEAL 78. SURE THINGS

Futile Willie
♠ A J 7 3
♡ J 9 7
◇ A K 8 6 4
♣ 4

Mrs. Guggenheim
♠ Q 10 9 6 4 2
♡ 8
◇ J 9 2
♣ A K 5

"I use the Rule of Two and Three," said Futile Willie. "When you play with me, all jumps are weak, Expect down two if vul, down three if not."

East, the Unlucky Expert, opened 1◇ on favorable vulnerability and West, Mr. Smug, made a Negative Double over Mrs. Guggenheim's 1♠ overcall, Willie made his favorite bid, a 2◇ cue bid, thinking to show a good hand with a big spade fit. East bid 2♡, South bid 2♠, West bid 4♡, and North bid 4♠. Smug had a fifth heart and bid a "level of trumps" 5♡.

"Nobody saves against me!" said Willie as he bid 5♠.

Everyone passed. Smug led the ♡K followed by the ♡Q. Googs ruffed and lost a finesse to East's ♠K. She ruffed East's ♡A return and lost a diamond at the end. Down one.

"Didn't Jack teach you to count, dear?" asked Willie.

What did he mean by that?

Googs could see 23 "points" in her own hand and dummy. That left 17 for East and West. By Trick 2, Smug had shown 5, the ♡KQ. The Expert needed the other 12 points for his opening bid.

Might his hand be ♠Kx ♡A10xx ◇Q10xx ♣QJ10? The only cards in doubt are one or two of the tens. So, to make 5♡, Googs needed to strip clubs and hearts, then feed a spade to East's ♠K. Endplayed? *Unlucky!*

DEAL 79. WHEN KANTAR MET JACOBY

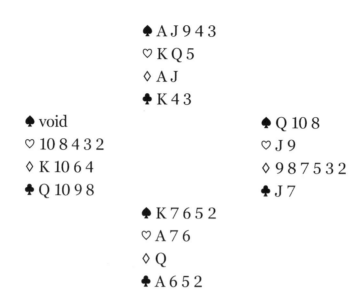

♠ A J 9 4 3
♡ K Q 5
◇ A J
♣ K 4 3

♠ void
♡ 10 8 4 3 2
◇ K 10 6 4
♣ Q 10 9 8

♠ Q 10 8
♡ J 9
◇ 9 8 7 5 3 2
♣ J 7

♠ K 7 6 5 2
♡ A 7 6
◇ Q
♣ A 6 5 2

North and South played Jacoby Forcing Raises and Roman Keycard Blackwood as most experts do now, South opened 1♠. North's 2NT showed a balanced forcing raise. South's 5♣ showed three. North's 5◇ asked for the ♠Q; South's 5♠ denied it. North's 6♣ was the Kantar Adjunct to RKB asking for third-round control. South's 6♠ denied it. Knowing that the ♣Q was missing, North passed, abandoning his grand slam hopes. Well bid, gentlemen, a fine demonstration of how to use your bidding toolkit!

West led the ♡3. South captured East's ♡J with the ♡A and led the ♠K. West started to think.

South turned to her and said, "Don't worry your pretty little head. If you follow, I'm claiming, as I can pick up your queen; a falsecard won't help. If you show out, I'm down one, as I have no discard for a club loser."

"Just a minute," said East, showing her hand, "I have queen-ten third." South's concession stood. Would you have conceded so fast?

Don't be so quick to claim or concede. Soldier on. After cashing both top spades, take the ◇A and ruff a diamond. Cash both top clubs, then play high hearts. If East doesn't ruff in, throw her in with another trump. With only diamonds left, she'll have to give you a ruff-sluff. You'll ruff in hand and discard dummy's last club. *Making 6♠*.

DEAL 80. A STEPPING STONE

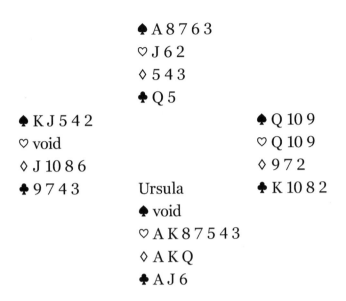

```
                    ♠ A 8 7 6 3
                    ♡ J 6 2
                    ◊ 5 4 3
                    ♣ Q 5
      ♠ K J 5 4 2                    ♠ Q 10 9
      ♡ void                        ♡ Q 10 9
      ◊ J 10 8 6                    ◊ 9 7 2
      ♣ 9 7 4 3        Ursula       ♣ K 10 8 2
                    ♠ void
                    ♡ A K 8 7 5 4 3
                    ◊ A K Q
                    ♣ A J 6
```

South opened a strong artificial 2♣ and rebid 2♡ **over** North's neutral 2◊ response. What would you bid next with the North hand? A case can be made for a natural positive 2♠, but North's raise to 3♡ was also reasonable.

It had the merit of promising at least three-card support. That enabled South to cue-bid 4♣ to show the ♣A in search of slam.

Cue bid? Really? What would she bid with five hearts and five clubs? At any rate, North thought it was a cue bid and cue-bid 4♠ in return to show the ♠A. South settled for 6♡ when North retreated to 5♡ over her 4◊ next.

West led the ◊J to declarer's ◊A. The ♡A brought the bad news in the trump suit. Yielding to the inevitable, South moaned, "Unlucky me," cashed the ♡K and surrendered a trick to East's ♡Q. East exited in diamonds and waited for a club trick. Down one.

Was defeat really inevitable?

Not if East had the ♣K and no more than three diamonds. After cashing two top hearts, all South needed was to cash three top diamonds and pray that East had no more diamonds left. Then upon being thrown in with the ♡Q, East could only put dummy in with a spade to let Ursula take a club finesse, or exit in clubs to take that finesse for her. Then 6♡ makes, and Ursula is unlucky no more.

DEAL 81. WHEN TRUMPS ARE THE TUXEDO

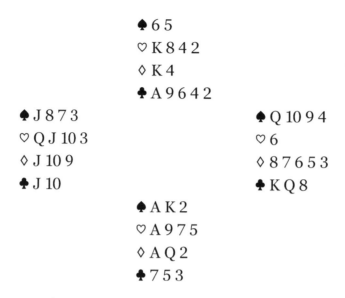

South opened 1NT and reached 4♡ via Stayman.

West led the ◊J. Declarer won dummy's ◊K and started cashing winners. First the ♡A and ♡K. Oops, the bad split meant that declarer suddenly had four losers, two hearts and two clubs. Down one.

Any way for declarer to have cope with the bad trump split? How would you try?

If you recognize the trump suit as the Tuxedo, you'll leave it in your closet until you need it for the Junior Prom. Strip the other suits first. Win the first seven tricks with three diamonds, two spades, a spade ruff in dummy and a club. Then feed the defenders two club tricks to reach:

With clubs gone, you can just play "second hand low" on any lead. If third hand plays a trump honor, win and "deep finesse" in trumps next to hold your trump losers to one. Don't touch the Tuxedo while you have any other suit to wear—uh, we mean, *play*.

DEAL 82. WHICH QUEEN-GUESSING RULE?

For decades, bridge players have proposed queen-guessing rules.

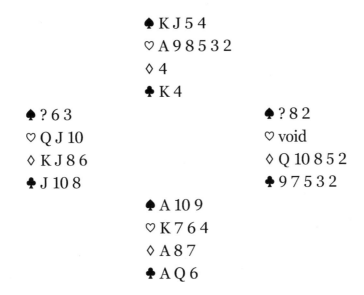

♠ K J 5 4
♥ A 9 8 5 3 2
⋄ 4
♣ K 4

♠ ? 6 3   ♠ ? 8 2
♥ Q J 10   ♥ void
⋄ K J 8 6   ⋄ Q 10 8 5 2
♣ J 10 8   ♣ 9 7 5 3 2

♠ A 10 9
♥ K 7 6 4
⋄ A 8 7
♣ A Q 6

South opened a 15-to-17 HCP 1NT and jump-accepted North's 2◇ transfer bid with his four-card support and super-maximum. Suddenly North felt himself to be in the slam zone. He bid 4♣ over South's 3♡ as a "Kickback" ask for key cards. When South replied 5♣ to show four, North put him in 6♡.

West led the ♣J, Declarer won in dummy and cashed the ♡A, learning the bad news.

"Bummer," thought South, "Now I have to guess the spade queen."

He tried to remember Danny's Queen-Guessing Rule, but he'd forgotten it. He guessed wrong and went down one.

Did you remember it and guess right?

Well, actually, it was Jim's Queen-Guessing Rule that applied: *Never guess a queen if you can make your opponents guess her for you.*

So strip the other suits. After East shows out on the ♡A, take the ◇A and ruff a diamond. Come to your ♡K and ruff your last diamond. Now ♣K, ♣A and ♣Q. Feed a trump trick to West and spread your hand. West must give you a ruff-sluff or break spades for you.

DEAL 83. THE MANATEE

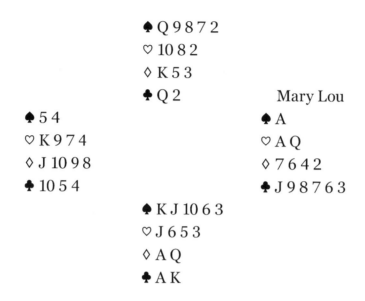

The late great Edgar Kaplan called a holding like West's ◊J1098 a "God-given sequence," and the ◊J is what West led against the mundane 1♠-2♠-3♠-4♠ auction.

Declarer won in hand and led the ♠6. East won and cashed the ♡A and ♡Q before shifting to the ♣7. South won and drew the last trump. He was able to discard one heart on dummy's ◊K but lost a heart to West's ♡K at the end. Down one.

Declarer had an illusion. Did you have the same one?

Some sailors look at manatees and see mermaids. Some bridge player look at queens and see beautiful creatures. The only beautiful creature here was Mary Lou. The ◊Q was a manatee. Were she a deuce, declarer might have seen the winning play easily.

Win the opening lead in hand and lead your last diamond, regardless of rank, to dummy's ◊K. Ruff dummy's last diamond and strip the ♠AK.

Now the table is set. Lead a trump in hope that the ♠A is singleton and the hearts are blocked. You're in luck. After East wins her bare ♠A and her two bare heart honors, she's endplayed. Having only minor-suit cards left, she must offer a ruff-sluff. Hello, Mary Lou! Goodbye heart.

Did you notice how two queens got swallowed?

DEAL 84. LOOK BUT DON'T TOUCH

♠ Q 6 5
♡ J 6 5 3
♢ K 6 5
♣ A K 7

♠ K 10 9 8 4 3
♡ A
♢ A 4 2
♣ 8 6 2

South opened 1♠ on favorable vulnerability and rebid 2♠ over North's 2♣ response. South rebid 2♠ and North put him in 4♠.

West led the ♡K to declarer's ♡A. With a loser in each minor, South needed to hold his trump losers to one. The ♠J was the pivotal card.

Declarer started trumps promptly at Trick 2 and tried to guess it. He guessed wrong. Down one.

Who do you think has the ♠J?

Who knows? You might try to figure out the distribution, but perhaps you can get a defender to break trumps for you. Yes, it is possible to strip the hands.

At Trick 2, cross to dummy in clubs and ruff a heart. Return to dummy with another club and ruff another heart. The ♢A and a diamond to the ♢K puts you back in dummy to ruff a third heart. East shows out. Does that mean you should finesse East for the ♠J?

No, you can do better than that. With eight tricks in the bag, simply exit in a minor. The defenders can win Tricks 9 and 10 with minor-suit honors, but then whoever wins Trick 10 will have to lead when you have ♠K109 in hand opposite ♠Q84 in dummy.

The defenders will guess the ♠J for you.

DEAL 85. A TRUMP STEP TO DUMMY

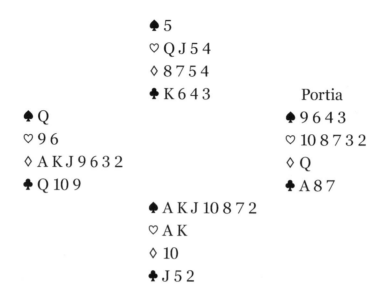

```
                    ♠ 5
                    ♡ Q J 5 4
                    ◊ 8 7 5 4
                    ♣ K 6 4 3           Portia
      ♠ Q                               ♠ 9 6 4 3
      ♡ 9 6                             ♡ 10 8 7 3 2
      ◊ A K J 9 6 3 2                   ◊ Q
      ♣ Q 10 9                          ♣ A 8 7
                    ♠ A K J 10 8 7 2
                    ♡ A K
                    ◊ 10
                    ♣ J 5 2
```

West opened 1◊. We wouldn't. Ely Culbertson stressed that an opening one-bid should deliver at least half an Honor Trick outside the suit. West's hand was nearly all offense and little defense. But 3◊ would not more keep South from jumping to 4♠ than East's 1♡ response to 1◊ did.

West led diamonds from the top but declarer ruffed the second and drew trump. He cashed both top hearts and led the ♣2. When West played the ♣9, he smiled, played dummy's ♣K and claimed, saying, "Dumping two clubs on dummy's hearts."

"Objection," said Portia, East. "Winning the ace and returning the eight. Down one."

Was there a way to unblock and use dummy's nice hearts?

Yes. For starters, take care to ruff the second diamond with the ♠7. Then cash the ♠A, and when West's ♠Q falls beneath it, only the ♠K and ♠J. Unblock the ♡AK, smile at Portia, feed her your carefully-preserved ♠2 and say, "Here's your retainer."

With only hearts and clubs left, the best she can do start clubs. No matter where the ♣A lies, that's the only trick the defenders can get. 4♠ makes. thanks to the precious ♠2.

DEAL 86. THINKING AHEAD

```
                    ♠ J 7 5 2
                    ♡ Q 5
                    ◊ A 7 4 2
        Carole       ♣ A Q 5        Dick
        ♠ Q 6 4                     ♠ void
        ♡ K 10 9                    ♡ 8 6 4 3 2
        ◊ Q J 10 3                  ◊ K 9 6 5
        ♣ J 10 3                    ♣ 9 8 6 2
                    ♠ A K 10 9 8 3
                    ♡ A J 7
        Danny        ◊ 8
                    ♣ K 7 4
```

When North eked out an artificial forcing raise of his 1♠ opening, South drove the Roman Keycard Blackwood Highway to 6♠. Carole, West, Danny's kibitzee, led the ◊Q. South looked at North and said, "Too bad you couldn't bid six hearts over my specific king-ask five notrump, or I'd have bid the good seven. But maybe I'll make seven on a finesse."

"Don't use the F-word with me," thought North silently. Then, turning her pretty little head upward she prayed "Please God, just let him make six."

South won dummy's ◊A at Trick 1 and without missing a beat led low to his ♠K. Whereupon Danny hummed Carole's favorite song wordlessly.

When East discarded, South took both top trumps and said, "Guess I'll have to fall back on the heart finesse. Dick, do you have the king?"

"There's that F-word again," thought North, while East said gleefully, "Fall back, baby!" When South crossed to dummy in clubs and led the ♡Q. Carole took the ♡K and cashed the ♠Q for down one.

Have you been paying attention? What tune was Danny humming?

"It's Too Late, Baby." It was too late for declarer as soon as he failed to ruff a diamond at Trick 2. Then, with club entries enough, he could strip both minors before feeding West her ♠Q for a forced heart exit to make 6♠.

DEAL 87. STUCK EVERYWHERE

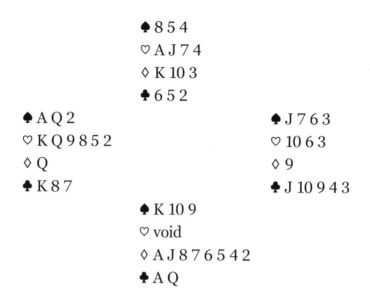

♠ 8 5 4
♡ A J 7 4
◊ K 10 3
♣ 6 5 2

♠ A Q 2
♡ K Q 9 8 5 2
◊ Q
♣ K 8 7

♠ J 7 6 3
♡ 10 6 3
◊ 9
♣ J 10 9 4 3

♠ K 10 9
♡ void
◊ A J 8 7 6 5 4 2
♣ A Q

South opened 1◊ and West overcalled 1♡. North bid 1NT. South bid 5◊. 3NT would have been better, but South knew neither that the diamonds would run nor that North had a second heart stopper.

West led the ♡K.

South played dummy's ♡A without pause for thought and then thought a long time (was he flipping a mental coin or uttering a silent "Eeny, meany, miney, mo"?) before discarding the ♣9. He drew trump with dummy's ◊K and finessed the ♣Q. It lost. He won West's club return, crossed to dummy's ◊10 and finesse the ♠K. That lost too. West cashed the ♠Q; down one.

Could you do better?

Sure you could! Ruff the ♡K with the ◊4 at Trick 1. Cash the ◊A and lead the ◊5 to dummy's ◊K. Then lead the ♠4 from dummy.

If East plays the ♠A, then your ♠K will score. If East plays the ♠J or ♠Q, your ♠K will drive out the ♠A; then your ♠10 will dislodge the remaining spade honor and your ♠9 will score. If East plays low, finesse the ♠9. He'll win but be endplayed in three suits. No matter how the cards lie, 11 tricks.

CHAPTER THREE

ADVANCED ELIMINATION DEALS

Here are some deals we think you will find a little more challenging. But by now, we're confident you will have no problem handling them.

DEAL 88. FALSECARDING

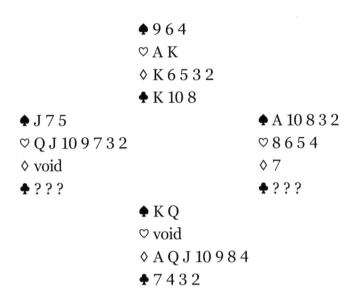

$\spadesuit$ 9 6 4
$\heartsuit$ A K
$\diamond$ K 6 5 3 2
$\clubsuit$ K 10 8

$\spadesuit$ J 7 5
$\heartsuit$ Q J 10 9 7 3 2
$\diamond$ void
$\clubsuit$? ? ?

$\spadesuit$ A 10 8 3 2
$\heartsuit$ 8 6 5 4
$\diamond$ 7
$\clubsuit$? ? ?

$\spadesuit$ K Q
$\heartsuit$ void
$\diamond$ A Q J 10 9 8 4
$\clubsuit$ 7 4 3 2

South opened 1$\diamond$, West overcalled 3$\heartsuit$, and North bid 3NT. When East bid 4$\heartsuit$, South bid 5$\diamond$ ending the auction. West led the $\heartsuit$Q.

Declarer discarded his $\spadesuit$KQ on dummy's $\heartsuit$AK and drew trump with his $\diamond$Q. He led the $\clubsuit$2, covering West's $\clubsuit$5 with dummy's $\clubsuit$8. Had it lost to the $\clubsuit$9, declarer planned to lead low to the $\clubsuit$K next, but it lost to the $\clubsuit$J. So he ruffed the spade return and led another club, covering West's $\clubsuit$6 with the $\clubsuit$10. This time West won the $\clubsuit$Q. Declarer lost three club tricks.

Down one. Good falsecard by East from $\clubsuit$ QJ9! Would you have been deceived by that falsecard?

We hope you wouldn't put yourself in position to be fooled. Discard the $\spadesuit$KQ on dummy's $\heartsuit$AK and ruff a spade high. Lead the $\diamond$Q to dummy's $\diamond$K and ruff another spade high. Lead the $\diamond$4 to dummy's $\diamond$5 and ruff dummy's last spade to complete the elimination.

Now lead s club. If West plays the $\clubsuit$A, you're home. Else cover West's card and if East wins, he's endplayed. Soon you'll hear West mutter to himself, 'Why didn't I underlead my ace of clubs at the start?'"

DEAL 89. ENCOURAGE, BUT WITH WHAT?

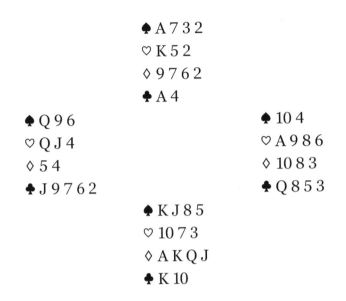

        ♠ A 7 3 2
        ♡ K 5 2
        ◊ 9 7 6 2
        ♣ A 4

♠ Q 9 6   ♠ 10 4
♡ Q J 4   ♡ A 9 8 6
◊ 5 4   ◊ 10 8 3
♣ J 9 7 6 2   ♣ Q 8 5 3

        ♠ K J 8 5
        ♡ 10 7 3
        ◊ A K Q J
        ♣ K 10

South opened 1NT and reached 4♠ via Stayman.

Declarer ducked West's ♡Q opening lead and East encouraged with the ♡8. West continued with the ♡J and declarer covered with dummy's ♡K. East won the ♡A and returned a diamond. Declarer won, led to dummy's ♠A and lost a finesse to West's ♠Q. But he lost only two hearts and one spade, so he made 4♠.

Could the defenders have done better?

Maybe. East should play the ♡9, not the ♡8, to Trick 1. Look how important it is for a defender to encourage by playing the highest of touching equals, thereby denying the card directly above.

East's ♡8 appeared to West to be from a suit headed by ♡A108 and thus deceived West into continuing hearts. But if West knows declarer has the ♡10, he will not continue hearts. The suit is "frozen": whoever plays the suit next loses a trick.

Can declarer counter the recommended *good* defense?

Yes, by winning West's shift and cashing the ♠AK. If the ♠Q doesn't drop, declarer can eliminate clubs and then diamonds. A defender who ruffs will have to lead a heart. If neither defender ruffs, declarer can lead a trump to endplay whichever defender has the ♠Q.

DEAL 90. COUNT AND DUCK

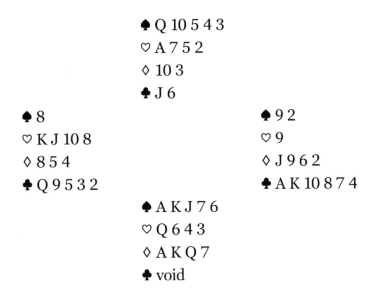

```
                    ♠ Q 10 5 4 3
                    ♡ A 7 5 2
                    ◊ 10 3
                    ♣ J 6
    ♠ 8                             ♠ 9 2
    ♡ K J 10 8                      ♡ 9
    ◊ 8 5 4                         ◊ J 9 6 2
    ♣ Q 9 5 3 2                     ♣ A K 10 8 7 4
                    ♠ A K J 7 6
                    ♡ Q 6 4 3
                    ◊ A K Q 7
                    ♣ void
```

After North raised South's 1♠ response to 2♠, East butted in with 3♣ on favorable vulnerability. Whereupon South's 4♣ and 5◊ cue bids and North's 5♡ cue bid led to 6♠ despite West's 5♣ raise.

West led the ♣3. Declarer ruffed East's ♣K and drew trumps. He cashed his high diamonds to discard the ♡2 from dummy. He took dummy's ♡A and led a heart back, hoping that East had the ♡K. When East showed out, declarer conceded down one.

Could South have held his heart losers to one?

The keen newspaper columnist Frank Stewart showed how.

If you ruff your last diamond in dummy, you will read West for his actual 1=4=3=5 distribution. So you can duck a heart and claim. If East wins, he has only clubs left and must lead one to give you a ruff-sluff. You'll ruff in hand, discard dummy's remaining low heart, and claim. If West wins, he must either lead from his ♡K or give a ruff-sluff similarly.

DEAL 91. PREEMPTIVE JUMP CRITICISMS

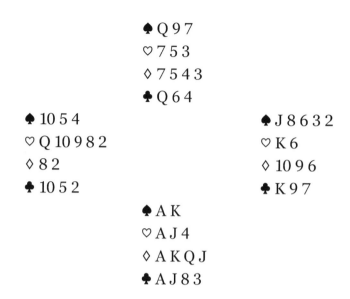

♠ Q 9 7
♡ 7 5 3
◊ 7 5 4 3
♣ Q 6 4

♠ 10 5 4
♡ Q 10 9 8 2
◊ 8 2
♣ 10 5 2

♠ J 8 6 3 2
♡ K 6
◊ 10 9 6
♣ K 9 7

♠ A K
♡ A J 4
◊ A K Q J
♣ A J 8 3

South opened an Omnibus and rebid 3NT over North's neutral 2◊ response, the usual auction for most who use modern methods.

West led the ♡10, top of an internal sequence. South captured East's ♡K. Short of dummy entries, South tried a sneaky ♣J, hoping West would win the ♣K and continue hearts. But East won the ♣K and his heart return sank the contract.

"You should have ducked the opening lead and ducked again," yelled North. "East will have no hearts when he wins the club king."

"But if West has the club king, I go down in a cold game," countered South defensively.

Who was right and who was wrong?

North was wrong. South's rebuttal was right, but his play wasn't. Best to win neither the first nor the third, but the *second* heart. Then he can cash six top tricks in diamonds and spades before exiting with his third heart.

After West cashes three hearts, he is endplayed. Either a spade to dummy's ♠Q or a club into declarer's tenace provides a ninth trick. Best to say nothing till after the session when you've had time to study the deal.

DEAL 92. DANGER ON THE HORIZON

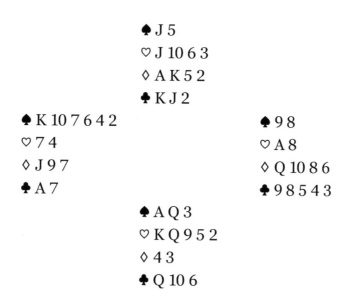

```
              ♠ J 5
              ♡ J 10 6 3
              ◊ A K 5 2
              ♣ K J 2
♠ K 10 7 6 4 2              ♠ 9 8
♡ 7 4                      ♡ A 8
◊ J 9 7                    ◊ Q 10 8 6
♣ A 7                      ♣ 9 8 5 4 3
              ♠ A Q 3
              ♡ K Q 9 5 2
              ◊ 4 3
              ♣ Q 10 6
```

South opened 1♡ in second seat. Playing Weak Single-Jump Overcalls, West bid 2♠ on favorable vulnerability. North might have cue-bid 3♠ to show a forcing heart raise, but he did better to bid 4♡, taking away a lead-directing double or absence thereof that the cue-bid raisers permit.

West led the ♣A and then the ♣7. Eager to draw trump, declarer won dummy's ♣K and the ♡J as though missing the ♡A and ♡Q.

But East wasn't buying it. He hopped with the ♡A and gave West a club ruff. West exited with the ◊7. When the spade finesse lost, declarer was down one.

A victim of an against-the-odds opening lead? Unlucky? Any way to overcome your bad luck?

Why not give it your best shot? If you can't keep West from getting a club ruff, perhaps you can end-play him after he gets it. So even before starting trump, try to extract his safe exits. At Tricks 3 and 4, cash the ◊AK and ruff a diamond. Now start trumps. West will get his club ruff, but if he's out of red cards (he will be!), he'll have to lead a spade up to your ♠AQ.

You'll make 4♡.

DEAL 93. GOING LOW TO AVOID A GUESS

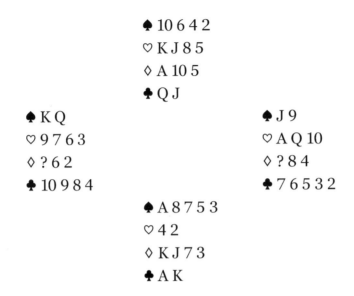

♠ 10 6 4 2
♡ K J 8 5
◊ A 10 5
♣ Q J

♠ K Q
♡ 9 7 6 3
◊ ? 6 2
♣ 10 9 8 4

♠ J 9
♡ A Q 10
◊ ? 8 4
♣ 7 6 5 3 2

♠ A 8 7 5 3
♡ 4 2
◊ K J 7 3
♣ A K

South opened 1♠ in fourth seat. North had his ♣J mixed with his spades and started to pull the 2♡ card from his bidding box, as they played Three-Way Reverse Drury, where two of the other major shows five-card support. Just in time he caught his sorting error and bid 2◊, showing a limit raise with four-card support. South bid 4♠.

West led the ♣Q to declarer's ♣A. The ♠A and another extracted the defenders' trumps. When West shifted to the ♡7, declarer tried dummy's ♡J. West took the ♡Q and ♡A and exits with the ♡10 to dummy's ♡K.

Declarer was left with a diamond guess. He guessed wrong. Down one.

Would you have guessed the diamonds right?

Why guess at all? Before leading two rounds of spades, cash the ♣K. When West wins and shifts to hearts, cover his card, Clubs having been stripped, East will be endplayed in three suits.

Making 4♠ without any guesses.

DEAL 94. DANGER HAND

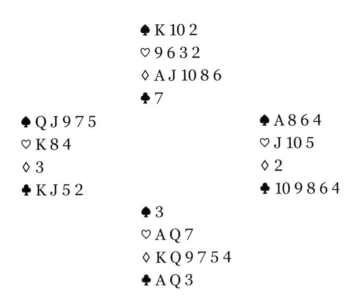

♠ K 10 2
♥ 9 6 3 2
♦ A J 10 8 6
♣ 7

♠ Q J 9 7 5
♥ K 8 4
♦ 3
♣ K J 5 2

♠ A 8 6 4
♥ J 10 5
♦ 2
♣ 10 9 8 6 4

♠ 3
♥ A Q 7
♦ K Q 9 7 5 4
♣ A Q 3

South opened 1♦ and West overcalled 1♠ on favorable vulnerability. North eschewed a Negative Double based on four hearts to the umpty in favor of a sensible 3♦ limit raise and East bid 4♠ preemptively to put South to the test. But South had ample values to pass the test with a cautious 5♦.

West led the ♠Q. South, who had just read our "Loser on Loser" book, covered with dummy's ♠K. He anticipated that East would win the ♠A and return a spade so he could discard the ♥7 on West's ♠J and the ♥Q on dummy's ♠10.

All that accomplished was to get a ♥J shift from East. The ♥Q lost to West's ♥K and declarer still had a late heart loser. Down one.

Unlucky, or ill-conceived? How would you have played?

First keep East, the danger hand, out. Duck the ♠Q. The spades are "frozen" and West may have no safe lead. West's best exit is the ♦3. Win and play the ♣A and ruff a club. Now lead the ♠K. East will cover; ruff and ruff your last club. Finally, another key play: lead the ♠10 and discard the ♥7, letting West win the ♠J with which his ♠Q opening lead marked him.

Zugzwang! Ruff-sluff or lead into the ♥AQ. You'll lose two spades but make ♦5.

DEAL 95. WITH A LITTLE BIT, WITH A LITTLE BIT

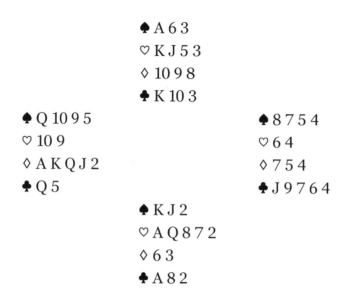

```
                    ♠ A 6 3
                    ♡ K J 5 3
                    ◇ 10 9 8
                    ♣ K 10 3
    ♠ Q 10 9 5                      ♠ 8 7 5 4
    ♡ 10 9                          ♡ 6 4
    ◇ A K Q J 2                     ◇ 7 5 4
    ♣ Q 5                           ♣ J 9 7 6 4
                    ♠ K J 2
                    ♡ A Q 8 7 2
                    ◇ 6 3
                    ♣ A 8 2
```

When West's 1◇ opening came round to him, South had more than enough to balance with 1♡ on favorable vulnerability. North eked out an invitational 3♡ raise and South gladly bid 4♡.

West led the ◇K, promising the ◇Q, then the ◇A, and shifted to the ♡10. Declarer finished trump, took dummy's ♠A and finessed the ♠J. West won the ♠Q and led the ◇J, announcing "Pinochle!"

"Wrong!" said East as declarer ruffed and conceded a club. "A pinochle scores only 40. We get 50 for down one."

Could you have done better? How would you play the spades?

We hope, *not at all*. At Trick 5, cash the ♣A and ♣K. Then lead dummy's ◇10. When East plays low, pitch your last club, a Loser-on-Loser play. West must offer a ruff-sluff in diamonds or a free finesse in spades.

With a little bit of luck, you'll make 4♡, losing three diamonds only.

What if West had falsecarded from ♣QJ5? Then he'd exit safely with the ♣J, but you could fall back on a spade Finesse as a Last Resort. We'd bet against West having ♠Qxx ♡109 ◇AKQJ2 ♣QJ5. Would you? Why?

DEAL 96. THOROUGHLY MODERN MOLLY DEMURS

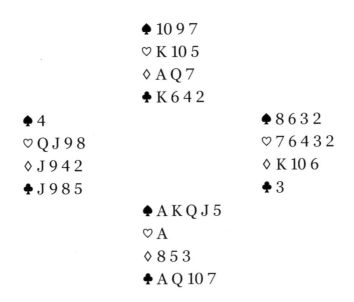

♠ 10 9 7
♡ K 10 5
♢ A Q 7
♣ K 6 4 2

♠ 4
♡ Q J 9 8
♢ J 9 4 2
♣ J 9 8 5

♠ 8 6 3 2
♡ 7 6 4 3 2
♢ K 10 6
♣ 3

♠ A K Q J 5
♡ A
♢ 8 5 3
♣ A Q 10 7

This deal occurred in a "boys against the girls" team game for a dollar an IMP, North, Thoroughly Modern Molly, opened 1♣. As they played Weak Jump Shifts, South, Thoroughly Modern Millie, responded 1♠ instead of 2♠. Molly rebid 1NT, Millie rebid 2♢, Two-Way New Minor Forcing, and 10 bids later (you'll have to ask Danny for an explanation) signed off in 6♠.

West led the ♡Q. Millie won the ♡A, drew trump pitching a club from dummy and cashed the ♣AK. Oops, East showed out. One last resort, a diamond finesse; when that lost, she went down one: minus 100.

"Flat board," said Millie. "Danny is South in the other room. He'll go down one too." Molly demurred. Well, do you think Danny could make 6♠?

We'll never know if Danny could make 6♠, but here's how *you* could, The ♡10 is the key. Before tackling clubs, cash a fifth spade pitching the ♢7 from dummy. When East shows out on the second club, cash dummy's ♢A, coming down to ♡K10 ♢Q ♣6 in dummy and ♢85 ♣Q10 in hand. West must keep ♡Jx ♣Jx to stop both suits. Play the ♡K and when West's ♡J doesn't fall, throw him in with it. He's endplayed and must lead into your ♣Q10.

Why did Molly demur?

"I know Danny," she said. "He's an old fuddy-duddy. He refuses to play any of the conventions. He'll jump-shift in spades, then support clubs, and Jim will have no trouble making the easy six clubs. We'll lose 16 IMPs."

DEAL 97. TWO FINESSES OR AN EXTRA CHANCE

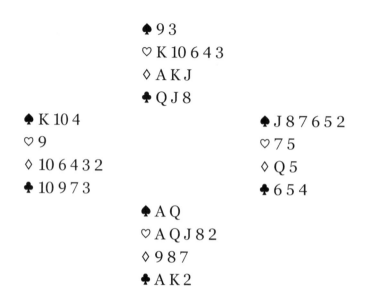

♠ 9 3
♡ K 10 6 4 3
♢ A K J
♣ Q J 8

♠ K 10 4
♡ 9
♢ 10 6 4 3 2
♣ 10 9 7 3

♠ J 8 7 6 5 2
♡ 7 5
♢ Q 5
♣ 6 5 4

♠ A Q
♡ A Q J 8 2
♢ 9 8 7
♣ A K 2

A good case can be made for trying to avoid 1NT openings with a five-card major (though it is often necessary to open 1NT with five hearts).

But with 21 points and a balanced hand one must normally open 2NT lest partner pass a 1♡ or 1♠ opening.

That spurred many experts to adopt the misnamed and troublesome "Puppet Stayman" for use in response to 2NT only, but simpler conventions that do not conflict with the more valuable Smolen Swaps are available.

South opened 2NT and jump-accepted North's Jacoby Transfer with his splendid support. North raised South's 4♡ to 6♡ on power.

West led the ♣10. Declarer won and drew trump. He tried the diamond finesse, No luck. He tried the spade finesse. That lost too. He slammed his remaining cards on the table and moaned, "If it weren't for bad luck, I'd have no luck at all."

His opponents and his kibitzer laughed. But was he right?

Not quite. Where there's trumps, there's hope. Think *elimination*. Draw trump, strip clubs, and play diamonds from the top. If West has the ♢Q, he's endplayed: *no spade finesse needed*. If East has the ♢Q, the spade finesse may still work later. Or (an extra chance) East's ♢Q may fall in the first two rounds. As here!

104

DEAL 98. AN UNUSUAL EXIT

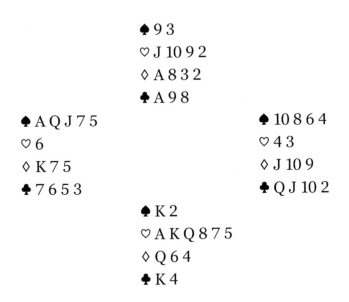

♠ 9 3
♡ J 10 9 2
◊ A 8 3 2
♣ A 9 8

♠ A Q J 7 5
♡ 6
◊ K 7 5
♣ 7 6 5 3

♠ 10 8 6 4
♡ 4 3
◊ J 10 9
♣ Q J 10 2

♠ K 2
♡ A K Q 8 7 5
◊ Q 6 4
♣ K 4

South opened 1♡ and North bid an invitational 3♡ over West's 1♠ overcall. South visualized slam opposite ♠A42 ♡96432 ◊8 ♣A652, but remembered Bob Hamman's maxim, "Don't play me for the perfect hand, I never have it," and settled for 4♡.

West's ♣7 opening lead rode to East's ♣J and South's ♣K. South drew trump and crossed to dummy's ◊A to lead low to his ◊Q. Tough luck, West won the ◊K and returned the ◊7 to East's ◊J. East's spade return meant down one.

Surely by now you can see a better play for ten tricks, can't you?

After the same opening lead, draw trumps and eliminate clubs. Then lead the ♠2! East can get in once to lead the ◊J through, but you'll let it ride to dummy's ◊A. Finally, you'll lead dummy's last spade to your ♠K.

When West wins the ♠A, he'll be endplayed. It's "Ruff-sluff or come to me in diamonds!"

DEAL 99. ASSUMPTIONS

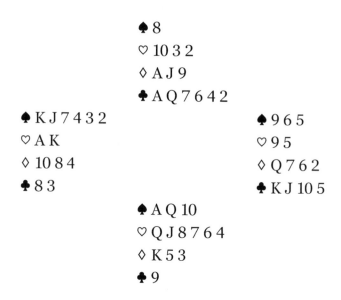

       ♠ 8
       ♡ 10 3 2
       ◊ A J 9
       ♣ A Q 7 6 4 2

♠ K J 7 4 3 2   ♠ 9 6 5
♡ A K   ♡ 9 5
◊ 10 8 4   ◊ Q 7 6 2
♣ 8 3   ♣ K J 10 5

       ♠ A Q 10
       ♡ Q J 8 7 6 4
       ◊ K 5 3
       ♣ 9

South opened 1♡ and West overcalled 1♠. North bid 2♣, then raised South's 2♡ rebid to 3♡. South bid 4♡.

West cashed both top trumps and aware of the dangers elsewhere. switched to the ♣8. Declarer was facing potential losers in spades and diamonds. A club finesse to discard a loser? A diamond finesse? A spade finesse? He tried them all and finished down one.

Was there any way to make this difficult contract?

Perhaps. Quite likely, West started with one or two low clubs and the ♠K. If he also had *either* the ◊Q *or* the ◊10, he could be stripped and thrown in successfully.

So, rise with the ♣A and ruff a club. Now lead the ♠Q, a queen sacrifice worthy of Paul Morphy. The best West can do is exit with a low diamond. You'll insert North's ◊9 to force an honor from East and then, if necessary, finesse West for the other honor.

Of course if West had a third club and led it when in with the ♠K, then you could ruff dummy's clubs good with an entry to spare.

DEAL 100. A DOUBLE HEADER

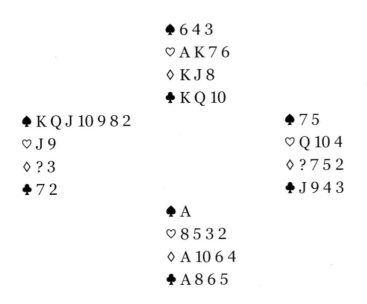

♠ 6 4 3
♥ A K 7 6
♦ K J 8
♣ K Q 10

♠ K Q J 10 9 8 2   ♠ 7 5
♥ J 9   ♥ Q 10 4
♦ ? 3   ♦ ? 7 5 2
♣ 7 2   ♣ J 9 4 3

♠ A
♥ 8 5 3 2
♦ A 10 6 4
♣ A 8 6 5

South opened 1♦, West overcalled 3♠ and North doubled.

In his good little book on Negative Doubles, Marty Bergen quotes Eddie Kantar as saying that no two players play them the same way. Bridge World Standard uses them through 3♠, the ACBL Yellow Card through 2♠, Marty through 3♣ (with his brainchild "Thrump Doubles" of 3♦, 3♥ and 3♠) and Danny's friend Mr. Mealymouth through 3♦. This North and South used them through 3♠.

North doubled. South grit his teeth and bid 4♥. North gambled 6♥. South bit his tongue and passed.

South captured West's ♠K opening lead with his bare ♠A. He cashed the ♥AK and prayed for a 3-2 split. When his prayers were answered, he guessed the ♦Q and guessed wrong. A trump loser put him down one.

Overambitious or underplayed?

Both, of course. Mike Lawrence suggested combining a dummy reversal with an endplay. At Trick 2, heart to the ♥K and ruff a spade. Heart to the ♥A and ruff another spade. Club to the ♣Q and stick East in with his high heart. Any exit gives you a twelfth trick.

Very nice! Thanks, Mike

DEAL 101. OUR FATHER

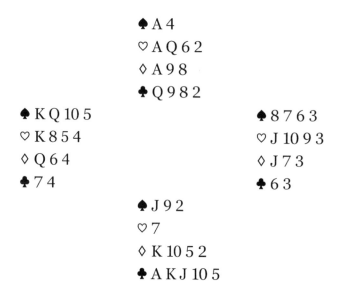

♠ A 4
♥ A Q 6 2
♦ A 9 8
♣ Q 9 8 2

♠ K Q 10 5   ♠ 8 7 6 3
♥ K 8 5 4   ♥ J 10 9 3
♦ Q 6 4   ♦ J 7 3
♣ 7 4   ♣ 6 3

♠ J 9 2
♥ 7
♦ K 10 5 2
♣ A K J 10 5

Were North the dealer, a simple 1NT-3NT auction would lead to an easy 3NT with North soon claiming 11 tricks on a heart lead and a 3-3 diamond split. But South dealt and opened 1♣, giving North an insoluble problem using currently popular methods. One simple solution is a 2♥ jump shift followed by club support. Better still, perhaps, is the Baron 2NT that shows a balanced 16-18 HCP with or without four-card majors. But as Yogi Berra might say, "Nobody bids that way any more, it's too effective."

When the smoke cleared, North responded 1♥ and gambled 6♣ over South's easy 2♣ rebid.

West led the ♠K. Declarer won dummy's ♠A, drew trump, said a silent "Hail Mary" and cashed both top diamonds. But in his hour of darkness, Mother Mary did not come to South: not even one diamond honor fell, much less two. He led a third diamond and conceded down one.

Anything better for South to have tried?

Yes. When "Hail Mary" offers such slim chances, try "Our Father." Win the ♠A and ♣A, then finesse the ♥Q. Throw a spade on dummy's ♥A and ruff a heart high. Lead low to dummy's ♣8 and ruff dummy's last heart.

Complete the elimination by feeding the ♠J to West's ♠Q. Then it's "Come to Papa!" As a ruff-sluff in spades will leave West with no chance, he'll shift to diamonds. By now, you know to play for split honors. Bingo!..

DEAL 102. GOOD HABITS

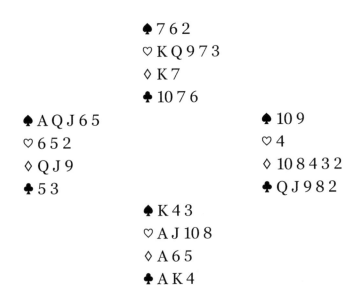

```
                    ♠ 7 6 2
                    ♡ K Q 9 7 3
                    ◊ K 7
                    ♣ 10 7 6
♠ A Q J 6 5                          ♠ 10 9
♡ 6 5 2                              ♡ 4
◊ Q J 9                             ◊ 10 8 4 3 2
♣ 5 3                              ♣ Q J 9 8 2
                    ♠ K 4 3
                    ♡ A J 10 8
                    ◊ A 6 5
                    ♣ A K 4
```

South opened 1♣, West overcalled 1♠, and lacking strength enough to bid 2♡, North made a Negative Double. South bid 4♡. A lucky auction!

West led the ◊Q. Declarer won and drew trumps ending in dummy. He led low to his ♠K. He lost three spade tricks now and a club trick later. Down one.

Could you have done better?

You could have done better just by developing good habits. *Strip the minors* if only to keep in practice. Look what happens when you lead to the ♠K now! If West takes his three spade tricks, he must give you a ruff-sluff. If he leads a low spade after winning the ♠A, East will win and cash a club, but then he must give you a ruff-sluff. Either way you make 4♡.

You would also have done better to open 1♡. Suppose West had stiffer standards for overcalling and had passed. Many fine players would. Or suppose West's diamonds had been ◊1098 instead of ◊QJ9. Few good players would overcall at all. Then North would respond 1♡ and become declarer in 4♡; a spade lead through your ♠K43 would wreck any chance to make 4♡.

Think about it! Any qualms you have about opening decent four-card majors should go out the window when you have a balanced hand too strong for 1NT but too weak for 2NT.

DEAL 103. THE SANDWICH 1NT

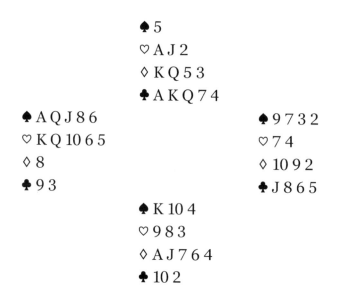

```
              ♠ 5
              ♡ A J 2
              ◊ K Q 5 3
              ♣ A K Q 7 4
♠ A Q J 8 6                    ♠ 9 7 3 2
♡ K Q 10 6 5                   ♡ 7 4
◊ 8                            ◊ 10 9 2
♣ 9 3                         ♣ J 8 6 5
              ♠ K 10 4
              ♡ 9 8 3
              ◊ A J 7 6 4
              ♣ 10 2
```

What do you need to overcall 1NT after your RHO responds to your LHO's opening? If you play it as natural, you need about half the deck in high cards in a balanced hand with stoppers in both suits. But when you have it, you ain't goin' nowhere, as your partner will be broke.

That's the logic behind "Sandwich Notrumps for *Takeout*," and West was pleased to bid one here to show 5-5 in the unbid suits after South responded 1◊ to North's 1♣. In the confused auction that followed, North correctly cue-bid hearts to show a stopper while forcing to game, but a confused South thought North was asking for a heart stopper rather than showing one. He missed the normal laydown 3NT and reached an iffy 6◊.

West led the ♡K. Prospects looked grim for South. He won dummy's ♡A, drew trump, and tried to run clubs to discard heart losers. Not surprisingly, West had only two clubs, so 6◊ failed.

.

Can you find a better plan?

Yes, if you appreciate the subtle value of the ♡J and ♠10. Take the ♡A, ◊A and ◊K, Then cash two clubs and ruff a club. Draw the last trump with dummy's ◊Q and discard hearts on dummy's ♣Q7.

Finally, lead dummy's ♠5 to your ♠10. West will win but be endplayed. Whether he leads hearts or spades, high or low, you'll score a ruff in that suit in one hand while setting up a trick in the other hand.

DEAL 104. WHEN ONE PARTNER HAS
ALL HIS SIDE'S HIGH CARDS

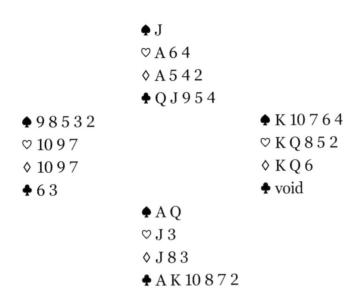

♠ J
♡ A 6 4
♢ A 5 4 2
♣ Q J 9 5 4

♠ 9 8 5 3 2
♡ 10 9 7
♢ 10 9 7
♣ 6 3

♠ K 10 7 6 4
♡ K Q 8 5 2
♢ K Q 6
♣ void

♠ A Q
♡ J 3
♢ J 8 3
♣ A K 10 8 7 2

East opened 1♠ on favorable vulnerability. South overcalled 2♣. Wanton preemption by West worked, as it kept his opponents from reaching the laydown 3NT and drove them into an iffy 5♣.

Declarer won the spade lead and drew trump. He led the ♢3 to dummy's ♢A, and the ♢2 to East's ♢Q. He discarded the ♢4 from dummy when East returned a spade. When the ♢Q did not fall beneath dummy's ♢A, declarer had to lose a heart trick. Down one.

Could you have done better?

Almost surely. After winning Trick 1 and drawing trump, cash your other high spade to discard the ♡4 from dummy. Now strip the hearts by cashing the ♡A and leading the ♡6. East can win but must either give you a ruff-sluff or break diamonds.

East's best bet is to shift to the ♢6, hoping you'll play low from your hand, but you can play the ♢J and pray. This time the ♢J is your best friend, and he will win. You'll make 5♣.

Notice that when one defender holds all, or nearly all, of his side's high cards, he's often susceptible to strip and throw-in plays. This fact applies to penalty doubles of opposing 1NT openings. Such doubles are not a good idea; they'll backfire when the doubler gets endplayed repeatedly.

DEAL 105. A HANDY UTENSIL

```
                    ♠ void
                    ♡ K Q J 4
                    ◊ K 7 5 3
                    ♣ Q J 8 4 2
♠ Q J 10 9 5 3                        ♠ 8 6 4 2
♡ 8 3                                 ♡ 7
◊ A J 9                               ◊ 10 8 6 4
♣ K 7                                 ♣ 10 9 6 3
                    ♠ A K 7
                    ♡ A 10 9 6 5 2
                    ◊ Q 2
                    ♣ A 5
```

South opened 1♡ and West overcalled 1♠. North and South played the usual kind of splinters, showing either a singleton or a void. Despite his wasted ♣K (well, perhaps not entirely wasted, as it was a trick), South cooperated with a 4♣ cue bid that showed the ♣A.

North bid 4NT, in their methods, Roman Keycard Blackwood. They both knew that a keycard ask by a splinterer at his next turn implies a void and excludes the ace of the short suit. South replied 5♠, showing two key cards and the ♡Q ... or so North thought. He did not know that length bringing the partnership total to 10 or more trumps counts as "queenth" (Danny's term for it). Puzzled, North bid 6♡, ending the auction.

West led the ♠Q. Declarer discarded dummy's ◊3 on his ♠A, drew trump, and lost a finesse to West's ♣K. Down one.

Any way to have avoided a club finesse?

Yes. Ruff the first spade high and come to your hand with the ♡10 to lead the ◊2. If West wins the ◊A, you'll eventually discard your low club on dummy's ◊K. If West ducks, you'll win dummy's ◊K, return to your hand with the ♡A and discard two diamonds from dummy on your ♠AK.

Then you'll feed your ◊Q to West's ◊A. He'll have to offer a ruff-sluff or lead away from his ♣K. This rare coup is called a *Morton's Fork*. Ask for one next time you eat at Morton's Steakhouse.

DEAL 106. A STEPPING STONE TO DECLARER'S HAND

```
                        ♠ J 10 7 3 2
                        ♡ 9 6 4
                        ◇ A K Q
                        ♣ A 6
    ♠ A K Q 9 8 4                        ♠ Void
    ♡ 7 5 3 2                            ♡ 8
    ◇ 7                                  ◇ 10 9 8 6 4
    ♣ 10 4                               ♣ K J 9 8 7 5 2
                        ♠ 6 5
                        ♡ A K Q J 10
                        ◇ J 5 3 2
                        ♣ Q 3
```

North opened 1♠ and South bid 3♡ over East's 3♣ Weak Jump Overcall. North raised to 4♡. West led the ♠ King, (showing the ♠Q in their methods).

West led the king, then ace of spades, East discarding a diamond and club. West switched to the nine of spades, East ruffed and declarer overruffed.

Declarer drew trumps and cashed the top diamonds. With no more trumps and no way back to the diamond jack, he had to lose two more tricks. Down one.

Was there a way to get back to the diamond jack, the tenth trick?

Perhaps. What if you discard the club ace while drawing trumps. After cashing the high diamonds, you can lead the small club from dummy. The position:

North: ♠ 10 7 ♡ -- ◇ -- ♣ 6   East:
                                            ♠ -- ♡ -- ◇ 10 ♣ K 8 (or ◇ 10 9 ♣ K)

South: ♠ -- ♡ -- ◇ J ♣ Q 3

East can win the king, but with nothing to return except a club or a diamond, he puts declarer back in hand to cash the tenth trick.

113

DEAL 107. DEAL 107 DOWN WITH THE PATRIARCHY

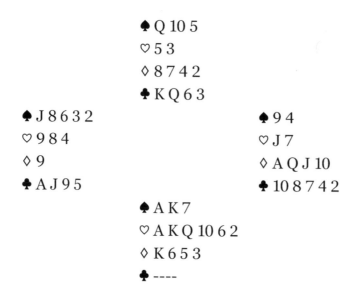

```
                         ♠ Q 10 5
                         ♡ 5 3
                         ◇ 8 7 4 2
                         ♣ K Q 6 3
         ♠ J 8 6 3 2                      ♠ 9 4
         ♡ 9 8 4                          ♡ J 7
         ◇ 9                              ◇ A Q J 10
         ♣ A J 9 5                        ♣ 10 8 7 4 2
                         ♠ A K 7
                         ♡ A K Q 10 6 2
                         ◇ K 6 5 3
                         ♣ ----
```

South opened 1♡ and North bid 1NT, forcing for one round. South bid 4♣, a self-splinter showing a 4♡ bid with club shortness. With the ♣KQ, North had no slam interest and bid 4♡. West led the ◇ 9.

The singleton diamond went to East's ace. Back came the diamond queen and West ruffed declarer's king. West exited a trump. Declarer, with two diamond losers, could go to dummy once and throw a loser on a club honor, but had no second entry. He finished down one.

Was there any way to dispose of those diamond losers?

Frank Stewart showed this a few years ago in one of his newspaper columns.

After the trump return, draw trumps and cash the spade ace. Sometimes a finesse is necessary. Play a spade to dummy's ten and lead the club king, unblocking the spade king. A king for a king.

The position now with West on lead:

North: ♠ Q ♡ -- ◇ 8 ♣ Q 6 3

West: ♠ J 8 6 ♡ -- ◇ -- ♣ J 9

South: ♠ -- ♡ 10 6 2 ◇ 6 5 ♣ --

West won the club ace but was endplayed. With only black cards remaining, West had to put declarer in the dummy. He discarded two diamond losers on the two black queens. Frank had "stepped" on West to reach dummy. Nice, Frank!

DEAL 108. FINDING A WAY OVER

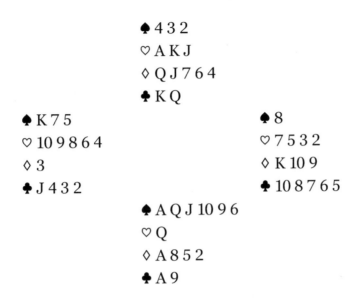

```
                    ♠ 4 3 2
                    ♡ A K J
                    ◇ Q J 7 6 4
                    ♣ K Q
    ♠ K 7 5                       ♠ 8
    ♡ 10 9 8 6 4                  ♡ 7 5 3 2
    ◇ 3                           ◇ K 10 9
    ♣ J 4 3 2                     ♣ 10 8 7 6 5
                    ♠ A Q J 10 9 6
                    ♡ Q
                    ◇ A 8 5 2
                    ♣ A 9
```

South open 1♠ and North bid 2◇. South "manufactured" a 3♣ high reverse preparatory to raising diamonds. He bid 4◇ over North's 3♠ preference. When North cue bid 4♡, South jumped to 6♠. West led the ♡ 10.

Declarer won the opening lead in dummy and took a trump finesse to his queen. West ducked, a good play to induce declarer to use another entry to repeat the trump finesse. Declarer went to dummy with a club and led another spade. East showed out. With no re-entry to dummy, he lost one diamond and one trump.

Was there a second entry to dummy for a diamond finesse?

Yes if you remove West's safe exit before repeating the trump finesse. After the ♠Q wins, go to dummy with a club and discard the ♣A on a high heart. Lead another trump and when East shows out, play the ace of trumps and lead another trump to reach this position:

West
♠ -- ♡ 9 8 6 ◇ 3 ♣ J 4 3

North: ♠ -- ♡ J ◇ Q J 7 6 4 ♣ Q

South: ♠ 10 9 6 ♡ -- ◇ A 8 5 2 ♣ --

West wins but is endplayed. He has to put declarer in the dummy. Declarer discards two diamonds on the two winners in dummy and can take a diamond finesse. Making six spades.

115

DEAL 109. A SNEAKY LEAD?

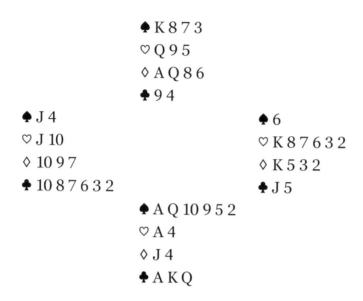

♠ K 8 7 3
♡ Q 9 5
◇ A Q 8 6
♣ 9 4

♠ J 4
♡ J 10
◇ 10 9 7
♣ 10 8 7 6 3 2

♠ 6
♡ K 8 7 6 3 2
◇ K 5 3 2
♣ J 5

♠ A Q 10 9 5 2
♡ A 4
◇ J 4
♣ A K Q

In third seat, Weak Two Bids can be "frisky," a good word to describe East's "favorable vulnerability" Weak 2♡ Bid here. South jumped to 3♠, a strong bid even for those whose single jump overcalls are ordinarily weak, as there are no weak jumps over opponents' weak bid,

North cue-bid 4♡ to show a strong raise than 4♠. South used Roman Keycard Blackwood to locate the missing key cards and gambled 6♠.

West led the ♡10. Jim thinks he was trying a tricky falsecard, but Danny thinks it more likely that his finger slipped.

South covered with dummy's ♡Q and captured East's ♡K with the ♡A. He drew trumps and cashed the ♣AKQ discarding the ♡5 from dummy. Now he led the ♡4 to dummy's ♡9, expecting East to win the ♡J. He beamed at her and cried, "Endplayed!"

But West had not yet turned his card to the trick. He pointed to her ♡J and said, "Oh really?" Then he led the ◇10. Declarer played low from dummy and East's ◇K took the setting trick.

Would you succumb to that tricky lead, or could you survive it?

Whether West led the ♡J or the ♡10 matters not so long at East has the ♡K for her Weak 2♡ Bid. Wouldn't you suppose she does? Play low from dummy at Trick 1 and the endplay that failed now works.

DEAL 110. TRUST YOUR EARS

Cover the bottom half of the page and see how you do.

♠ A J 6
♡ A K J 7
◊ 7 6 4
♣ A 7 3

♠ K 5 4
♡ 9 2
◊ A J
♣ K J 10 9 5 2

With both sides vulnerable, partner doubles West's 3◊ opening (we don't know if we would) and you bid 6♣. West leads the ◊K and East follows with the ◊2. Take it from here.

NO PEEKING!

How did you play the trumps? How did you play the major suits? Did you make your slam? If not, blame North for his offshape double before he can blame you for your play.

West probably doesn't have a singleton heart or spade, else he might have led one. So you'll do well to play him for a singleton club. After leading to dummy's ♣A and picking up East's ♣Qxx on the way back, you must tackle the majors.

How? Easy! As East now has only majors left, lead the ♡9 and let it ride if not covered. East will win but he's endplayed in both majors. You get a free finesse. Losing one heart only. Twelve tricks.

West: ♠1072 ♡63 ◊KQ109853 ♣8   Eest: ♠Q983 ♡Q10854 ◊2 ♣Q64

117

DEAL 111. WRONG IMPLEMENT

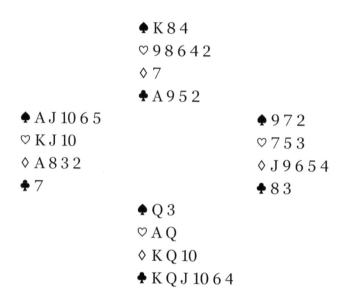

```
                    ♠ K 8 4
                    ♡ 9 8 6 4 2
                    ◊ 7
                    ♣ A 9 5 2
♠ A J 10 6 5                         ♠ 9 7 2
♡ K J 10                             ♡ 7 5 3
◊ A 8 3 2                            ◊ J 9 6 5 4
♣ 7                                 ♣ 8 3
                    ♠ Q 3
                    ♡ A Q
                    ◊ K Q 10
                    ♣ K Q J 10 6 4
```

When you can pass the opponents out in a partscore, there are no weak preempts. So no matter how he might play it in the direct seat, after West's 1♠ and two passes, South's 3♣ jump was strong.

3NT being shaky despite her spade stopper, North bid 5♣. All passed and West led the ◊A. Seeing nothing better to do, he continued the ◊2.

Thinking elimination, declarer discarded the ♠4 from dummy. Right plan but wrong implementation. He drew trump and led the ♠3 up. West won the ♠A and returned a spade. When the heart finesse lost, down one.

Do you know which implement South needed to implement his plan?

That's right, a fork. Specifically, a Morton's Fork. Declarer must save both of dummy's low spades. Discard a heart on the second diamond and draw trump. *Now* lead the ♠3.

If West takes his ♠A, dummy's ♠K will provide a discard for the ♡Q. If West ducks, dummy's ♠K wins. South comes to his hand with a trump to discard a spade on his high diamond and feeds the ♠Q to West.

West is endplayed and must lead into declarer's ♡AQ. A tasty morsel.

DEAL 112. HOLD YOUR CARDS BACK

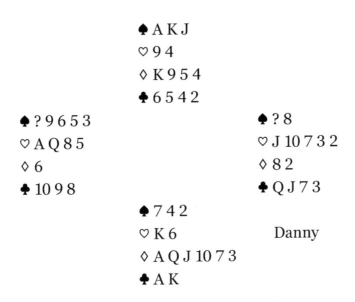

♠ A K J
♡ 9 4
◊ K 9 5 4
♣ 6 5 4 2

♠ ? 9 6 5 3
♡ A Q 8 5
◊ 6
♣ 10 9 8

♠ ? 8
♡ J 10 7 3 2
◊ 8 2
♣ Q J 7 3

♠ 7 4 2
♡ K 6   Danny
◊ A Q J 10 7 3
♣ A K

South opened 1◊ and North bid 2◊, forcing at least one round, a limit raise or better. South bid 5◊ (3NT would be better) and West led the ♣ 10.

What could go wrong, thought the declarer? The ♠Q and the ♡A both offside? He saw Danny, sitting Southeast. scribbling notes. Doubleton queen? Danny loves those deals for his books with Jim. Declarer drew trumps and both finesses lost, down one.

Was there a way to increase your chances?

Declarer does better by playing along elimination lines. After winning the opening lead, draw trumps, cash the other high club and play a spade to the ace. Ruff a club. Cross to dummy with a trump and ruff the last club. The position:

North: ♠ K J ♡ 7 6 ◊ 9 ♣ --

West
♠ ? 8 6 ♡ A Q ◊ -- ♣ --

East
♠ ? ♡ J 10 8 5 ◊ - ♣ -

South ♠ 7 4 ♡ K 4 ◊ Q ♣ --

Declarer leads a spade. When West plays low, play the ace! East's queen falls!
"How could you see in my hand," asks East? "Was I holding my cards too open?"

If West had the ♠Q, declarer was about to endplay West with it to lead a heart. This just covered the chance of East having a doubleton queen.

DEAL 113. A BENT FORK

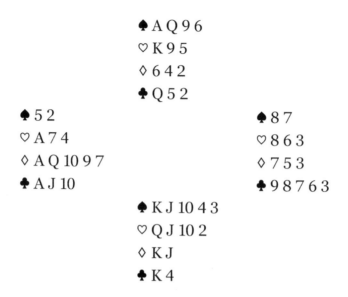

♠ A Q 9 6
♡ K 9 5
◇ 6 4 2
♣ Q 5 2

♠ 5 2
♡ A 7 4
◇ A Q 10 9 7
♣ A J 10

♠ 8 7
♡ 8 6 3
◇ 7 5 3
♣ 9 8 7 6 3

♠ K J 10 4 3
♡ Q J 10 2
◇ K J
♣ K 4

South opened 1♠. West overcalled 2◇ and North made a limit raise, jumping to 3♠. South's 4♠ ended the auction and West led the ♠ 2.

Declarer finished trumps and led to the ♡K and back to the ♡Q. West won and exited in hearts. Declarer recognized a possible Morton's Fork in clubs. He cashed his last heart and discarded a worthless diamond from dummy.

Then South led the ♣4, West ducked. Dummy's ♣K won, but when West captured declarer's ♣K with the ♣A on the next round, he continued the ♣J. South had to ruff and lead diamonds from his hand. Down one.

Had declarer discarded a club from dummy on the fourth heart, West would have won the first club and returned a club with the same result.

Good try, right idea, but what went wrong?

The Morton's Fork got bent when declarer cashed the last high heart. He wasn't ready to make a discard. If declarer leads his low club first, the Morton's Fork spears the last juicy piece of steak. West must duck, so dummy's ♣Q wins.

Declarer returns to his hand with a trump and cashes his last heart to discard a club. Then he feeds his ♣K to West and West is endplayed.

DEAL 114. GOING THE WRONG WAY

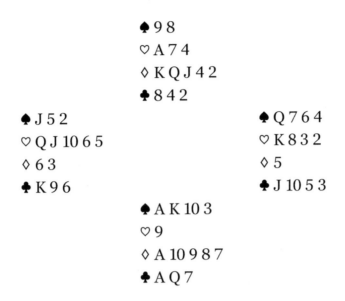

```
                    ♠ 9 8
                    ♡ A 7 4
                    ◇ K Q J 4 2
                    ♣ 8 4 2
     ♠ J 5 2                        ♠ Q 7 6 4
     ♡ Q J 10 6 5                   ♡ K 8 3 2
     ◇ 6 3                          ◇ 5
     ♣ K 9 6                        ♣ J 10 5 3
                    ♠ A K 10 3
                    ♡ 9
                    ◇ A 10 9 8 7
                    ♣ A Q 7
```

South opened 1◇ and North bid 2◇, which they played as an "Inverted Minor" raise, forcing for one round. They played Roman Keycard Gerber in strong minor-suit auctions, and North's 4NT reply to 4♣ showed two keys and the ◇Q. When North replied 5◇ to South's Specific King-Ask 5♣ next, South settled for 6◇. West led the ♡ Queen.

Declarer won West's ♡Q opening lead in dummy. Thinking along elimination lines, he ruffed a heart, cashed his top spades, ruffed a spade, ruffed dummy last heart and drew the last trump. Then he led the ♠10. If West covered, he'd throw a club from dummy, a loser-on-loser play to endplay West. The club finesse was a last resort.

Alas, East had the fourth spade and the club finesse lost. Down one.

Do you see a better plan?

Look at those spade spots! Between the two hands, you have ♠AK1098. After winning the ♡A, ruff a heart high, cross to dummy in trump, ruff dummy's last heart, lead another trump to dummy, and lead the ♠9. If East covers, win the ♠A and lead to the ♠8, a defender can win, but then you'll throw two clubs on the ♠K10. If East plays low, let the ♠9 ride to West, who will then be endplayed.

You won't need a club finesse. Not even as a last resort.

DEAL 115. CAN'T DODGE IT

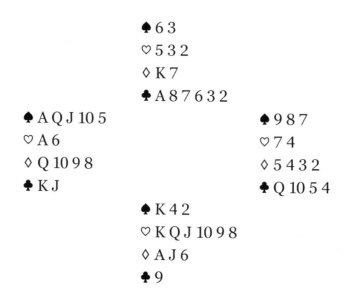

```
                    ♠ 6 3
                    ♡ 5 3 2
                    ◊ K 7
                    ♣ A 8 7 6 3 2
♠ A Q J 10 5                          ♠ 9 8 7
♡ A 6                                 ♡ 7 4
◊ Q 10 9 8                            ◊ 5 4 3 2
♣ K J                                 ♣ Q 10 5 4
                    ♠ K 4 2
                    ♡ K Q J 10 9 8
                    ◊ A J 6
                    ♣ 9
```

When West's 1♠ opening came round to him, South wasn't quite strong enough to jump to 3♡, so he balanced with 2♡. West rebid 2♠, and when North took the push to 3♡, South gladly bid 4♡.

West led the ♡A and then the ♡6.

In search of a tenth trick, South led to dummy's ◊K and the finessed the ◊J. West won the ◊Q and exited in diamonds. Declarer later lost two spade tricks. Down one.

Reading West for nearly all the high cards, could you endplay him?

Yes! After winning the second trump, strip the clubs: ♣A, club ruff, ◊K, and a second club ruff. Too bad the clubs don't split 3-3! But then you can cash the ◊A and lead the ◊J. When West plays the ◊Q, discard a spade from dummy. That's only the second trick for the defense.

West dare not cash the ♠A, else your ♠K will be a tenth trick for you. So he'll do best to lead his last diamond. When he does, let him win it, the third trick for the defense, discarding spades from both hands.

Now West is endplayed. He must give you two tricks: one with your ♠K (a trick you didn't expect to get), another by a spade ruff with dummy's last trump. That's West's third trick, the last for the defense. Whew!

DEAL 116. THRUST AND PARRY

```
              ♠ J 6
              ♡ Q J 10 7 2
              ◊ K 10 6
              ♣ A 4 3
♠ A Q 10 9 5 2            ♠ 8 7 3
♡ void                   ♡ 8 5 4
◊ 9 8 7 4                ◊ 5 3 2
♣ K Q J                  ♣ 10 9 7 5
              ♠ K 4
              ♡ A K 9 6 3
              ◊ A Q J
              ♣ 8 6 2
```

Not wanting to face the awkward rebid problem that a 1♡ opening would bring after a 1♠ response, South opened 1NT. But it was West who held the spades and overcalled 2♠. North-South had just the convention they needed to cope: *Reuben Transfers* starting with 2NT, so North bid 3◊ to show hearts. (Pity the downtrodden Lebensohlers who bid 3♡ in the other room and had no chance in 4♡ at all!)

Here South jumped to 4♡ and West led the ♣K. Declarer saw two losers in each black suit looming unless he could strip the hand. He won the ♣A and drew trump.

West saw the endplay coming. He dumped the ♣QJ. South stripped diamonds and led a club. He turned to West and asked, "Got the ten too?"

But West discarded, so East took two clubs and shifted to spades. West took two spades. Down one.

Could you have overcome West's good defense?

Yes. Don't rely on West's having the ♣10. Once he discards a club honor, cash three diamonds ending in dummy and feed him dummy's ♠J. He can take two spades and his other club honor but then he must give you a ruff-sluff.

Either way you make 4♡.

DEAL 117. PAY ATTENTION

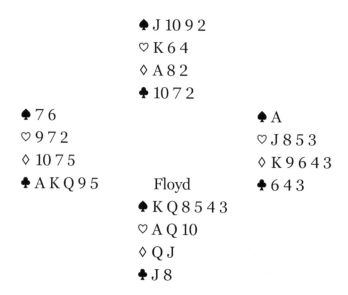

```
              ♠ J 10 9 2
              ♡ K 6 4
              ◇ A 8 2
              ♣ 10 7 2
♠ 7 6                           ♠ A
♡ 9 7 2                         ♡ J 8 5 3
◇ 10 7 5                        ◇ K 9 6 4 3
♣ A K Q 9 5      Floyd          ♣ 6 4 3
              ♠ K Q 8 5 4 3
              ♡ A Q 10
              ◇ Q J
              ♣ J 8
```

After three passes, South opened 1♠ on adverse vulnerability. West overcalled 2♣ and North raised to 2♠. Overvaluing his quack-laden hand a bit, and perhaps too eager to bid a vulnerable game at IMPs, South invited game with 3♠ and North bid 4♠.

West led the ♣K and declarer seemed to stare blankly at dummy for two minutes before dummy said, "Floyd, play a card already for God's sake."

Floyd shook his head from side to side, mumbled "Sorry," and followed suit to this and to the ♣A that followed, He ruffed the ♣Q next and drove out the ♠A promptly. Later he lost a diamond finesse. Down one.

How would you declare 4♠? Not that we think you'd have bid it.

Because West passed as dealer, we trust you would mark East with both the ♠A and the ◇K. Your only legitimate chance is to strip and endplay East if his ♠A is singleton.

So, cash the ♡A and ♡Q, then lead to dummy's ♡K. Lead the ♠J from dummy as though thinking to finesse against a missing ♠Q. Maybe East will duck with a doubleton ♠A. It could happen. Here East has no choice but to win his singleton ♠A. Zugzwang!

CHAPTER FOUR

DEFENSE

Time to take the other seats and defend.

DEAL 118. SEE YOU LATER, ALLIGATOR

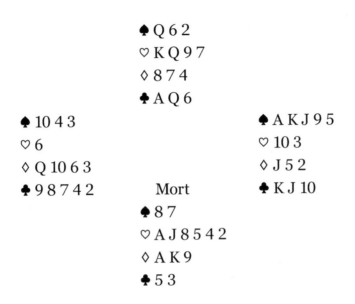

```
                    ♠ Q 6 2
                    ♡ K Q 9 7
                    ◊ 8 7 4
                    ♣ A Q 6
    ♠ 10 4 3                       ♠ A K J 9 5
    ♡ 6                            ♡ 10 3
    ◊ Q 10 6 3                     ◊ J 5 2
    ♣ 9 8 7 4 2      Mort          ♣ K J 10
                    ♠ 8 7
                    ♡ A J 8 5 4 2
                    ◊ A K 9
                    ♣ 5 3
```

East overcalled North's 1♣ opening with 1♠ and South reached game via 2♡-3♡-4♡. West led the ♠3, low from honor-third. East won the ♠J, cashed the ♠K and tapped declarer with the ♠A.

Declarer drew trump with the ♡Q and ♡A as East followed up the line with the ♡3 and ♡10, and up the line with the ◊2 and ◊4 when declarer cashed the ◊A and ◊K.

West covered declarer's ◊9 with the ◊10 and fingered the ♣9 to lead to the next trick but East overtook with the ◊J.

South showed his hand and turned to East, saying, "See you later, Alligator! You can either lead up to dummy's clubs or give me a ruff-sluff."

Could the defense have prevailed? Whose fault that 4♡ made?

This ending featured a Crocodile Coup. *Either* defender could have starved the crocodile to death. West by observing East's carding, up the line in diamonds showing an odd number, and rising with the ◊Q on the third round. East by dropping the deadly ◊J on the second round to avoid being thrown in with it.

Then the defenders could listen to South, Post-Mortimer Snide, scold North: "Is chivalry dead? Why didn't you bid notrump to protect your black queens? Don't you know Danny's *Rule of Three Queens*?"

DEAL 119. DON'T COUP YOURSELF

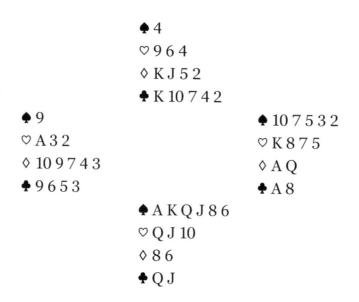

```
                    ♠ 4
                    ♡ 9 6 4
                    ◊ K J 5 2
                    ♣ K 10 7 4 2
♠ 9                                    ♠ 10 7 5 3 2
♡ A 3 2                                ♡ K 8 7 5
◊ 10 9 7 4 3                           ◊ A Q
♣ 9 6 5 3                              ♣ A 8
                    ♠ A K Q J 8 6
                    ♡ Q J 10
                    ◊ 8 6
                    ♣ Q J
```

Downgrading his hand for its preponderance of queens and jacks, South rebid only 2♠ after North responded 1NT to his 1♠ opening.

West led the ◊10. East captured dummy's ◊J with the ◊Q and shifted to the ♡5. West won the ♡A and returned the ♡3 to East's ♡K.

Declarer won the third heart and cashed the ♠AK, getting the bad news. He abandoned trumps to lead the ◊8 and ducked West's ◊9. East overtook with the ◊A perforce and tapped declarer with the thirteenth heart.

Declarer led the ♣Q. If East let it win, the next club would endplay him. So he won the ♣A while he still had a low club for safe exit. It mattered not. South overtook the ♣J with dummy's ♣K and led the ♣2 from dummy, saying, "I think this must be good by now."

East said, "No, I'm ruffing." He was down to ♠1075 and ruffed with the ♠7. South had ♠QJ8 and overruffed with the ♠8. Making 2♠.

Were the defenders helpless to beat 2♠?

No. East could beat it by cashing the ♣A and exiting in clubs when in with the ◊A. To execute a trump coup, declarer must shorten his trumps. *Don't do it for him!* Against better defense, declarer can overtake his club honor with dummy's ♣K and ruff a club, but he lacks another dummy entry to finish the job. Down one.

DEAL 120. TIMING, OFFENSE AND DEFENSE

♠ J 7 5
♡ A Q 5 2
◇ J 10 4 3 2
♣ 3

South	West	North	East
1◇	1♠	double*	2♠
3◇	3♠	5◇	All Pass

You

♠ A K Q 9 4 2
♡ 9 7
◇ void
♣ J 10 7 6 5

*Negative Double
(showing four or more hearts)

Playing Patriarch Opening Leads, you start with the ♠K, showing the ♠Q. How should you continue?

NO PEEKING

The point of leading the king instead of the usual ace is that when you continue with the ace, partner will know you have AKQ. No other order of leading from the three tops conveys the same information. So if you led the ♠A to Trick 2, pat yourself on the back for playing the suit correctly.

But you're not just playing one suit, you're trying to beat a contract. On this deal, your best chance to beat 5◇ is not to run South out of trumps but to set up a heart trick for partner before declarer can endplay him.

You must do it now, for you know from the bidding that a second spade won't cash. Shift to the ♡9 immediately. If instead you lead the ♠A, declarer eliminates both black suits by ruffing, and feeds partner his trump trick, for the two unseen hands are:

♠ 10 8 3
♡ K 10 8 4 3
◇ A
♣ 9 8 4 2

♠ 6
♡ J 6
◇ K Q 9 8 7 6 5
♣ A K Q

DEAL 121. STILL YOUR LEAD

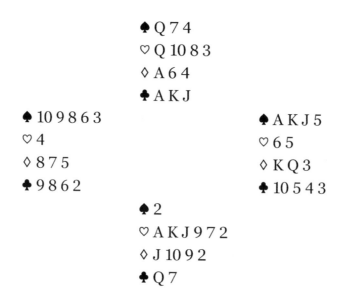

```
                    ♠ Q 7 4
                    ♡ Q 10 8 3
                    ◊ A 6 4
                    ♣ A K J
    ♠ 10 9 8 6 3                   ♠ A K J 5
    ♡ 4                            ♡ 6 5
    ◊ 8 7 5                        ◊ K Q 3
    ♣ 9 8 6 2                      ♣ 10 5 4 3
                    ♠ 2
                    ♡ A K J 9 7 2
                    ◊ J 10 9 2
                    ♣ Q 7
```

South opened 1♡. Playing Jacoby Forcing Raises, he was required to bid a "shortness-showing" 3♠ over North's 2NT response. North, who would still have enough to force to game if his ♣K were the ♣2, cue-bid 4◊ and then 5♣, the right order to elicit a 5◊ cue-bid showing the ◊K in return, but honored South's 5♡ signoff.

West led the ♠10. South mumbled "Shoulda opened a Weak Two," and played low from dummy. When the ♠10 held, West continued the ♠6.

South ruffed, drew trumps, cashed three clubs and ruffed dummy's last spade. Then, having stripped the hand, he let the ◊J ride to East and claimed his precarious 5♡ contract, as East was endplayed.

Who erred, if anyone?

West erred by failing to shift to diamonds at Trick 2. If not eager for this shift, East could overtake the ♠10 with the ♠J to continue spades.

South erred by failing to cover the ♠10 and prevent that shift.

Was South's decision to open 1♡ an error too? We wouldn't call it that, even if we prefer a Weak 2♡ Bid. No matter where we draw the line, there will be borderline hands too close to call. Culbertson's criterion of half an Honor Trick outside the suit is relevant, but it's a postulate, not a theorem.

DEAL 122. OH, WHAT IS THAT I SEE YONDER COMING, COMING, COMING?

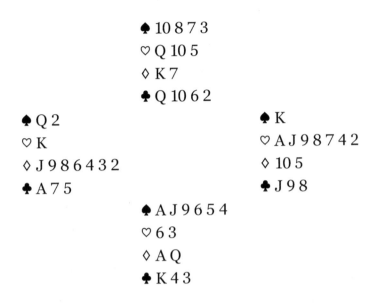

```
                    ♠ 10 8 7 3
                    ♡ Q 10 5
                    ◊ K 7
                    ♣ Q 10 6 2
    ♠ Q 2                              ♠ K
    ♡ K                                ♡ A J 9 8 7 4 2
    ◊ J 9 8 6 4 3 2                    ◊ 10 5
    ♣ A 7 5                            ♣ J 9 8
                    ♠ A J 9 6 5 4
                    ♡ 6 3
                    ◊ A Q
                    ♣ K 4 3
```

East opened 3♡. South bid 3♠ and North raised to 4♠. West led

the ♡K and shifted to the ◊9. Declarer won dummy's ◊K and led the ♠3, capturing East's ♠K with his ♠A Then he cashed the ◊A.

The stage was set. Declarer fed a spade to West's ♠Q. West exited with the ◊J, but declarer ruffed in dummy diamonds while shedding a club from his hand. That was one loser, a club loser, gone.

A club to the ♣K drove out West's ♣A, but that was only the third trick for the defense. When the ♣J fell on the third round, dummy's ♣10 provided a discard for declarer's remaining heart, a second loser gone. Making 4♠.

Could the defenders have beaten 4♠?

Look what happens if West jettisons the ♠Q under the ♠A. Now declarer can finish trumps with dummy's ♠10 and strip the diamonds, but cannot keep East from getting in with the ♣J. Two club losers and two heart losers mean down one.

West should be able to see what's coming if he *doesn't* throw his ♠Q under the wheels. Did you?

Kudos to South for starting spades from his hand! The problem is harder for West to see when he mistakes his queen for a commoner.

DEAL 123. DON'T HELP OUT

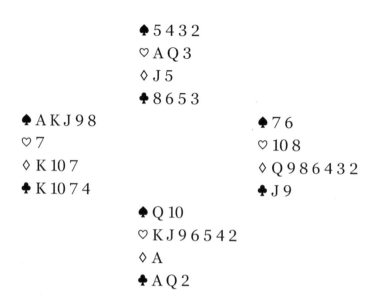

♠ 5 4 3 2
♡ A Q 3
◇ J 5
♣ 8 6 5 3

♠ A K J 9 8
♡ 7
◇ K 10 7
♣ K 10 7 4

♠ 7 6
♡ 10 8
◇ Q 9 8 6 4 3 2
♣ J 9

♠ Q 10
♡ K J 9 6 5 4 2
◇ A
♣ A Q 2

South opened 1♡. West overcalled 1♠, North raised to 2♡ and South bid 4♡. West cashed both top spades and continued with the ♠J.

Declarer ruffed, unblocked the ◇A, crossed to dummy's ♡A, ruffed a diamond, and drew the last trump with dummy's ♡Q, taking care all the while to preserve the ♡2 just to stay in practice.

He led dummy's last spade, struck his forehead with his palm and cried, "Dummkopf! I must have had this mixed with my clubs!" as he played the ♣2. "I hope I haven't revoked."

"Uh, no, that actually is a club. But thanks for not ruffing," said West, as he raked in the trick with the ♠8. Then, unwilling to offer a ruff-sluff, he exited in clubs, right up to declarer's ♣AQ. Ten tricks; 4♡ made.

West was a very nice gentleman, but could he have defended better?

Yes. After cashing the first two spades, West should have exited passively in trump. By leading a third spade, he helped declarer strip the hand.

Looking at it in a different way ... by leading the ♠J, West wasted a precious exit card, using it before he needed it.

DEAL 124. AVOIDING THE ENDPLAY – PUNCH AND COUNTERPUNCH

<pre>
                    ♠ A 4
                    ♡ A K J 6 5
                    ◊ A 6 4
                    ♣ A 6 4
   ♠ K Q 10 6 5 3   ♠ 9 8 7
   ♡ 8   ♡ 10 4
   ◊ Q 9 2   ◊ J 10 5 3
   ♣ K J 8   ♣ 10 9 5 2
                    ♠ J 2
                    ♡ Q 9 7 3 2
                    ◊ K 8 7
                    ♣ Q 7 3
</pre>

West opened 1♠ in third seat. With a bit too much for a mere 2♡ overcall, North doubled for takeout, then wisely refrained from jumping to 4♡ over South's 2♡ advance. North cue-bid 2♠ and South jumped to 4♡.

West led the ♠K against 4♡.

Declarer won in dummy and drew trump. Seeing four potential losers, he cashed the ◊A and ◊K, then fed the ♠J to West's ♠Q. West cashed the ◊Q, but then had to break clubs or offer a ruff-sluff. 4♡ made.

Could West have beaten 4♡?

Probably ... by dropping the ◊Q under the ◊K. Then, suspecting that West started with ◊Q2 doubleton, declarer would probably still stick him in with the ♠Q. Imagine South's chagrin when West produces the ◊9 to exit safely and East wins the ◊10 to lead the ♣10 through. Why only "probably"?

Because a better declarer would not fall into that trap. Whether West falsecards the ◊Q or keeps it, South should exit in diamonds. keeping the ♠J as a feeder for an endplay *after* the ♣A has been dislodged.

Thanks to Mike Lawrence for this theme.

DEAL 125. COUNTING THE POINTS

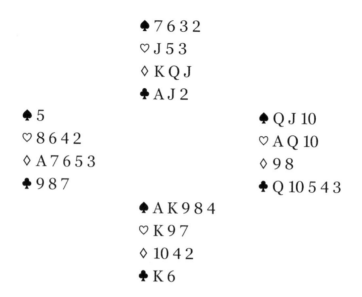

```
                    ♠ 7 6 3 2
                    ♡ J 5 3
                    ◇ K Q J
                    ♣ A J 2
     ♠ 5                              ♠ Q J 10
     ♡ 8 6 4 2                        ♡ A Q 10
     ◇ A 7 6 5 3                      ◇ 9 8
     ♣ 9 8 7                          ♣ Q 10 5 4 3
                    ♠ A K 9 8 4
                    ♡ K 9 7
                    ◇ 10 4 2
                    ♣ K 6
```

In a team game at IMPs, East opened 1♣ in third seat on favorable vulnerability. South overcalled 1♠ and based on the favorable placement of his ♣K and ♡K, he bid 4♠ over North's invitational 3♠, ending the auction.

West's ♣9 opening lead rode to declarer's ♣K. He cashed two top trumps and led the ◇2. West hopped up with the ◇A to continue clubs.

Declarer won dummy's ♣A and ruffed off East's ♣Q. Then he cashed dummy's two diamond honors. Not wanting to be endplayed, East refrained from ruffing. She threw a club, but then declarer threw her in with her ♠Q.

As East pondered her next lead, South said, "I'll save you time and trouble. I've counted the points. You have both the ♡A and the ♡Q. You need them for your opening bid even in third seat. So you must either give me a ruff-sluff or break hearts. Believe me, Honey, I won't get the hearts wrong. Making four." Then he showed his hand.

South, a well-known pro, was the club's manager. He summoned the director, who said, "Next match starts in six minutes. Making four. Score it up and compare with your teammates." Was that ruling right?

No. East leads the ♡Q, a "surrounding" play. South wins the ♡K but East still has ♡A10 behind dummy's ♡J5 and gets *two* tricks. Down one. A director should never make a ruling involving a player who can fire him.

DEAL 126. THE EXCUSE

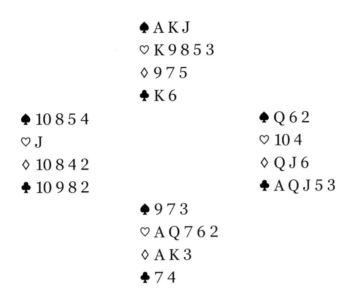

♠ A K J
♥ K 9 8 5 3
♦ 9 7 5
♣ K 6

♠ 10 8 5 4
♥ J
♦ 10 8 4 2
♣ 10 9 8 2

♠ Q 6 2
♥ 10 4
♦ Q J 6
♣ A Q J 5 3

♠ 9 7 3
♥ A Q 7 6 2
♦ A K 3
♣ 7 4

South opened 1♥ as dealer. Playing Jacoby Forcing Raises, he bid a "Fast Arrival Shows Trash" 4♥ (denying extra shape or strength) over North's 2NT artificial balanced forcing raise.

West led the ♣10 and continued with the ♣2 when it held. East won the ♣A and exited safely with the ♥4.

Declarer took his two aces, drew the last trump with dummy's ♥K, returned to his hand with the ♦K and exited with the ♦3.

East won and was endplayed: ruff-sluff or up to dummy's ♠AKJ.

4♥ made.

West was keeping score and toted up the score for the rubber. "How many chances do you need to find the winning play?" he asked while reaching for his wallet to pay his losses.

"It's late and I'm tired," said East. "At this time of night I need two."

Should West accept this excuse?

No. It's a lame one. East *had* his two chances. At Trick 3, when he should have shifted to the ♦Q, Then at Tricks 4 and 6 when he could have unblocked his two diamond honors.

DEAL 127. THE QUEEN IS DEAD …

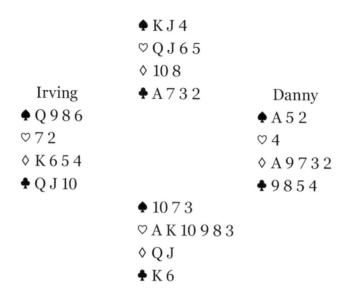

```
                        ♠ K J 4
                        ♡ Q J 6 5
                        ◊ 10 8
        Irving          ♣ A 7 3 2         Danny
        ♠ Q 9 8 6                         ♠ A 5 2
        ♡ 7 2                             ♡ 4
        ◊ K 6 5 4                         ◊ A 9 7 3 2
        ♣ Q J 10                          ♣ 9 8 5 4
                        ♠ 10 7 3
                        ♡ A K 10 9 8 3
                        ◊ Q J
                        ♣ K 6
```

This deal occurred in a Knockout Teams. West was a successful businessman whose wife hired Danny to partner—secretly, so as not to wound his fragile ego. His name was Irving but he was known as *Duke*.

After a 1♡ - 3♡ - 4♡ auction, West led the ♣Q. South won the ♣K, cashed the ♡A, led to dummy's ♣A and ruffed a club with the ♡8. He drew the last trump with dummy's ♡J and ruffed dummy's last club. Strip and endplay on the horizon!

South tried to slip the ◊J by West, but he rose with the ◊K, saying, "Not through the Iron Duke," a pun on his name that often drew guffaws.

He got off lead with the ◊4. Danny won the ◊A. South, one of the stronger pros, turned to him, smiled her most fetching smile, and said, "Endplayed!"

Danny exited silently with the ♠2. South played the ♠3, and captured West's ♠Q with dummy's ♠K. Then declarer led the ♠J to Danny's ♠A and claimed the rest. Making 4♡ and earning a "Nicely played!" from her client.

But could better defense have beaten her?

Yes. Irving thought his ♠Q was dead, but her maidservants. the ♠986, offered ample life support. Any one of them beats 4♡. When your queen is surrounded by the king-jack, play the lowest card that will force the jack if you have any. *"Third hand high" doesn't apply when it's futile.*

DEAL 128. WHAT'S HE SAYING?

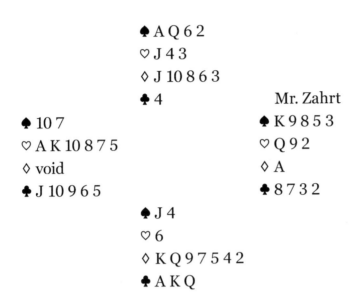

```
              ♠ A Q 6 2
              ♡ J 4 3
              ◊ J 10 8 6 3
              ♣ 4                    Mr. Zahrt
  ♠ 10 7                            ♠ K 9 8 5 3
  ♡ A K 10 8 7 5                    ♡ Q 9 2
  ◊ void                           ◊ A
  ♣ J 10 9 6 5                      ♣ 8 7 3 2
              ♠ J 4
              ♡ 6
              ◊ K Q 9 7 5 4 2
              ♣ A K Q
```

South opened 1◊ on favorable vulnerability, West overcalled 1♡ and North made a Negative Double promising four spades. East raised to 2♡ promising three-card support, South rebid 3◊, West bid 3♡ showing a sixth heart, and North's jump to 5◊ ended the auction.

West led the ♡K, as his partner, an old man named Mr. Zahrt, insisted on old-fashioned leads and signals. East followed with the ♡2.

"What's he saying?" wondered West. "I know he has three hearts from his raise, so he's not showing count. I know his remaining hearts are the queen and nine, so he's not showing weakness. What's left? It must be suit preference."

Whereupon West closed his eyes and the ♣J. Declarer cashed three top clubs discarding dummy's hearts, led the ◊2 and turned to East, saying, "I'm finessing you for the ace of trumps."

Before West could play a card, Mr. Zahrt folded his cards and said, "I have it, finesse wins. You make five diamonds."

What was East saying? Or was he just speaking Zahrtese?

Mr. Zahrt had been stripped and end-played, forced to give a ruff-sluff or lead from the ♠K. His ♡2 simply discouraged hearts and urged West to shift. The obvious ♠10 shift takes him off the endplay and beats 5◊.

137

DEAL 129. WHEN DANNY MET FREDDY

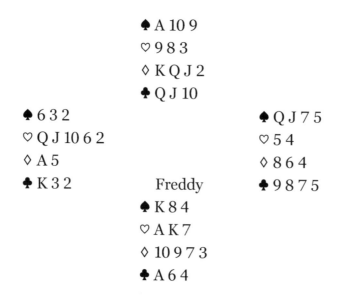

♠ A 10 9
♡ 9 8 3
◊ K Q J 2
♣ Q J 10

♠ 6 3 2
♡ Q J 10 6 2
◊ A 5
♣ K 3 2

Freddy

♠ Q J 7 5
♡ 5 4
◊ 8 6 4
♣ 9 8 7 5

♠ K 8 4
♡ A K 7
◊ 10 9 7 3
♣ A 6 4

Danny remembers what his friend Wall Street George said to Bob Hamman when Bob was trying to eke out a living at rubber bridge in 1963:

"How foolish you are, heading for the strongest game in the house when you could do as I do, seeking out pigeons in the weakest games!"

"George," said Bob, pointing to his intended victims, "You don't understand. Those are *my* pigeons."

About 15 years later, Fred Hamilton, fresh from winning a Bermuda Bowl, walked into the rubber bridge club where Danny played. Was he Danny's pigeon? Not exactly. Danny loved to have Fred at his table because at last he had a partner with whom to play bridge as it should be played. So what if it was only one chukker out of every three?

On this deal, Fred opened 1◊ and bid 3NT after West overcalled 1♡ and Danny cue-bid 2♡ to show a forcing raise. Fred won Trick 1 with the ♡A, drove out the ◊A, and won the next heart honor with the ♡K. On the third and fourth diamonds, West discarded black deuces. Was he toast?

Yes. Fred cashed two spades and threw West in with a heart. After taking three hearts, West was endplayed and had to lead from ♣K3. 3NT made. To avoid the Hamilton Beach Toaster, West had to bare the ♣K. *In tempo*, neither huddling nor twitching, else Fred would have picked it up.

DEAL 130. SHORT SUITS FIRST

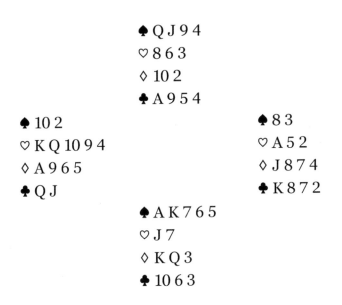

♠ Q J 9 4
♡ 8 6 3
♢ 10 2
♣ A 9 5 4

♠ 10 2
♡ K Q 10 9 4
♢ A 9 6 5
♣ Q J

♠ 8 3
♡ A 5 2
♢ J 8 7 4
♣ K 8 7 2

♠ A K 7 6 5
♡ J 7
♢ K Q 3
♣ 10 6 3

North raised South's 1♠ opening to 2♠ after West overcalled 2♡ and took the push to 3♠ when East's 3♡ raise came round to him.

The ♡K won Trick 1, the ♡A won Trick 2, and South ruffed the third heart. He appeared to have one diamond and two clubs to lose for down one. He drew trump with the ♠A and ♠J. Then he led the ♢2 to his ♢K.

West won the ♢A and shifted to the ♣Q. Declarer won dummy's ♣A, cashed the ♢Q and ruffed his last diamond in dummy. Now a low club from dummy gave East two losing options. Rise with the ♣K and smother West's ♣J, turning declarer's ♣10 into a winner? Or let the club ride to West's ♣J, forcing West to lead a red suit and give declarer a ruff-sluff.

Yes, declarer did well to make 3♠, but could the defenders have beaten it?

Yes, with a little forethought. West might have anticipated that by continuing hearts, he was helping declarer strip the hand. He'd have done better to attack clubs while he still had safe exit-cards in other suits to avoid the strip-and-throw-in that loomed.

Then upon winning the ♢A, West can unblock the ♣J and exit safely. When West gets in with his ♢A, he can cash his club trick and exit safely in diamonds. In strip-and-endplay deals, passive defense often fails.

DEAL 131. WHAT DID CHARLIE DO?

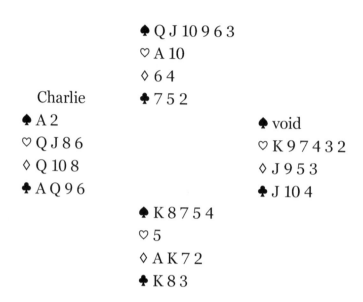

```
                        ♠ Q J 10 9 6 3
                        ♡ A 10
                        ◊ 6 4
         Charlie        ♣ 7 5 2
         ♠ A 2                              ♠ void
         ♡ Q J 8 6                          ♡ K 9 7 4 3 2
         ◊ Q 10 8                           ◊ J 9 5 3
         ♣ A Q 9 6                          ♣ J 10 4
                        ♠ K 8 7 5 4
                        ♡ 5
                        ◊ A K 7 2
                        ♣ K 8 3
```

After South's 1♠ opening on favorable vulnerability and West's takeout double, North's 4♠ jump ended the auction.

West led the ♡Q to dummy's ♡A. Declarer ruffed dummy's ♡10 and led another trump. West, fearing an endplay, rose with the ♠A and exited with the ♠2 while East threw hearts.

South cashed two top diamonds and led the ◊2, discarding the ♣2 from dummy. What happened next?

Trick question! You may not have been around inattentive defenders as long as we have. so you might not guess. Half a minute went by before South looked at West and said, "Your turn, Charlie."

Yes, it was Charlie's lead. What would you lead?

Another trick question. We hope you wouldn't have faced that problem. If you've unblocked the ◊Q earlier, East can win the ◊J and lead the ♣J through to beat the contract.

Poor Charlie. He should have gotten off the train at the Scollay Square station when he had the chance.

DEAL 132. ONCE MORE WITH FEELING

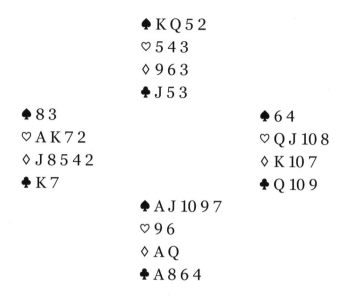

```
              ♠ K Q 5 2
              ♡ 5 4 3
              ◇ 9 6 3
              ♣ J 5 3
♠ 8 3                          ♠ 6 4
♡ A K 7 2                      ♡ Q J 10 8
◇ J 8 5 4 2                    ◇ K 10 7
♣ K 7                          ♣ Q 10 9
              ♠ A J 10 9 7
              ♡ 9 6
              ◇ A Q
              ♣ A 8 6 4
```

South opened 1♠ with both sides vulnerable at IMPs. Playing "Bergen Raises," North jumped to 3♣ to show a standard raise to 2♠ with a fourth spade. Frustrated at being unable to bid 3♣ as a game try, South took the bull by the horns and jumped to 4♠.

Playing Patriarch Opening Leads, West led the ♡A, showing the ♡K while denying the ♡Q. East dropped the ♡Q, showing the ♡J and requesting an underlead. West obliged with the ♡2, his original fourth highest, standard practice. East won the ♡10 and tapped declarer with the ♡8.

Declarer knew she needed lots of luck. She cashed the ♣A, crossed to dummy's ♠Q, finessed the ◇Q successfully and cashed the ◇A. She crossed to dummy's ♠K, praying for 2-2 trumps, and ruffed dummy's last diamond. Then she lost a club trick.

What would you play next as West?

It doesn't matter. If you kept the blocking ♣K, it doesn't matter, as whichever red card you lead will let declarer discard dummy's last club and ruff in hand to make 4♠. If you dropped the ♣K under declarer's ♣A, it doesn't matter either, as partner will cash the master club, the setting trick.

All that matters is whether you unblocked as you must.

DEAL 133. IMAGINE …

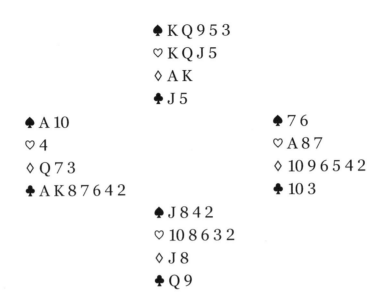

West opened 1♣ and North doubled for takeout. South bid 1♡. West rebid 2♣. North jumped to 3♡ and everyone passed.

West cashed ♣AK and everyone followed. He switched to a diamond. Declarer won and drew trumps. After conceding a spade, he had the rest. Making ♡3.

East was unhappy. "Didn't you want to beat three hearts?" he asked.

How would you have beaten 3♡ if you were West?

Visualize the layouts that can let you beat the contract, and cater to them. One is partner's possible ♡A10xx. You needn't do anything to cater to that.

A second is partner's possible ♡A10x. To cater to that you need only lead a third club. If declarer ruffs with one of dummy's trump honors, partner can duck and eventually get two trump tricks. Otherwise partner can ruff with the ♡10 and beat 3♡ that way.

Yet another is partner's possible ♡Axx and doubleton spade. To cater to that you must also lead a third club. Partner may have no heart high enough to promote, but he can discard a spade and upon winning the ♡A he can lead to your ♠A to get a spade ruff.

DEAL 134. NOT ALL FINESSES ARE EQUAL

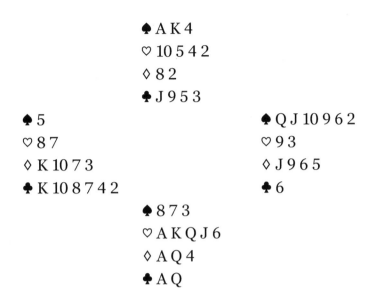

```
                    ♠ A K 4
                    ♡ 10 5 4 2
                    ◊ 8 2
                    ♣ J 9 5 3
      ♠ 5                            ♠ Q J 10 9 6 2
      ♡ 8 7                          ♡ 9 3
      ◊ K 10 7 3                     ◊ J 9 6 5
      ♣ K 10 8 7 4 2                 ♣ 6
                    ♠ 8 7 3
                    ♡ A K Q J 6
                    ◊ A Q 4
                    ♣ A Q
```

South dealt and deemed his hand a bit too strong for a 2NT opening. So he opened an Omnibus 2♣. We agree. North made the usual neutral 2◊ response, and South started to reach for his 2NT bidding card. He caught himself just in time, for East had not yet called. On favorable vulnerability, she threw in a monkey-wrench 2♠.

With three low spades, South reconsidered his rebid. He bid 3♡. Seeing no "scientific" way to probe for a grand slam, North raised to 6♡.

West led the ♠5 against 6♡. East dropped the ♠Q under dummy's ♠K.

Declarer drew trump with the ♡A and ♡K. Then he cashed the ♣A and led the ♣Q. He was glad he had read Jim's book, *"The Finesse as a Last Resort,"* when West won the ♣K and East discarded the ♠9.

"Endplayed!" thought West. A club exit would let declarer win a proven finesse of dummy's ♣9. But might East have the ◊Q for her trashy overcall? So he shifted to the ◊3. Curtains! Soon declarer took the rest of the tricks and chalked up +1430.

Hopeless task or bad guess? Could West have survived the endplay?

No guess at all. Upon winning the ♣K West had a count: South was 3=5=3=2 or 2=5=4=2. The ♣J was always good for one discard but a second discard on the ♣9 would do South no good at all. By exiting in clubs, West could wait to score his ◊K and beat 6♡ regardless of the ◊Q.

DEAL 135. A HOT POTATO

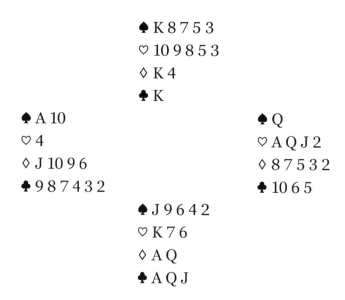

      ♠ K 8 7 5 3
      ♡ 10 9 8 5 3
      ◇ K 4
      ♣ K

♠ A 10   ♠ Q
♡ 4   ♡ A Q J 2
◇ J 10 9 6   ◇ 8 7 5 3 2
♣ 9 8 7 4 3 2   ♣ 10 6 5

      ♠ J 9 6 4 2
      ♡ K 7 6
      ◇ A Q
      ♣ A Q J

Using a "good 12 to bad 15" notrump range, South opened 1♣. North's "weak freak" 4♠ jump ended the auction.

West led the ♡4. East won the ♡A and returned the ♡Q. South covered with the ♡K and West ruffed. Reading the ♡Q as suit preference for diamonds. and having a "God-given" sequence from which to lead, West led the ◇J to Trick 3.

South won, played the rest of his diamonds and clubs from the top, throwing hearts from dummy, led the ♠2 and prayed. When East's ♠Q fell beneath West's ♠A, South thanked whichever God to whom he had prayed and claimed: "Whichever minor you lead, I'll ruff in dummy and pitch my losing heart."

"I thought your heart queen was suit-preference, dear," said West.

"Don't you remember, honey," answered East. "We agreed to play upside-down signals. Including suit-preference. The better to confuse opposing declarers who never think to ask. I wanted a club shift."

Who was right?

Neither. The key to beating 4♠ was avoiding an endplay. It's seldom right to sit on the fence with the master trump when it's bare. Get it out of your hand like a hot potato. Before you get your fingers burned.

DEAL 136. WHAT KIND OF VEGETABLE
IS THIS ANYWAY?

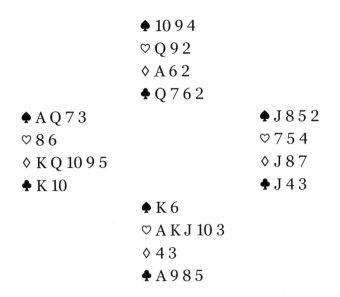

```
                  ♠ 10 9 4
                  ♡ Q 9 2
                  ◊ A 6 2
                  ♣ Q 7 6 2
♠ A Q 7 3                        ♠ J 8 5 2
♡ 8 6                           ♡ 7 5 4
◊ K Q 10 9 5                     ◊ J 8 7
♣ K 10                          ♣ J 4 3
                  ♠ K 6
                  ♡ A K J 10 3
                  ◊ 4 3
                  ♣ A 9 8 5
```

Playing the "Equal Level Conversion" convention that permits a takeout double of a major with five diamonds and four of the other major even with neither extra strength nor club support, West doubled South's 1♡ opening. North bid 2♡ and accepted South's pushy 3♣ game invitation.

West led the ◊Q, a prophylactic against the Bath Coup, and when declarer played low from dummy, East dropped the ◊J as requested. Declarer won West's ◊9 continuation with dummy's ◊A, led low to his ♣A, cashed the ♡A, crossed to dummy's ♡9 and ruffed dummy's last diamond.

Now declarer led the ♣5. West won the ♣K and was endplayed: break spades or offer a ruff-sluff with a fourth diamond. Soon declarer was able to draw the last trump and claim his contract.

Any way for the defenders to have stopped him?

Yes. Had West been aware of the looming endplay, he would have dropped the ♣K like ... did we ever use the phrase "hot potato"?

If West dumps the ♣K, then East will win the ♣J and lead a spade through to beat the contract. Did we hear anyone say, "But what if declarer, not East, had the ♣J?"

That's possible, even likely, and dumping the ♣K could cost 30 points or 1 IMP. But it's a worthwhile investment to *beat the contract.*

DEAL 137. BRAHMS' LULLABY

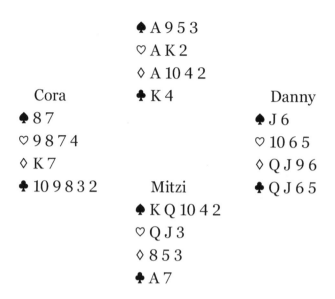

```
                    ♠ A 9 5 3
                    ♡ A K 2
                    ◊ A 10 4 2
       Cora         ♣ K 4         Danny
    ♠ 8 7                      ♠ J 6
    ♡ 9 8 7 4                  ♡ 10 6 5
    ◊ K 7                      ◊ Q J 9 6
    ♣ 10 9 8 3 2    Mitzi      ♣ Q J 6 5
                    ♠ K Q 10 4 2
                    ♡ Q J 3
                    ◊ 8 5 3
                    ♣ A 7
```

Mitzi Mezzosoprano had the endearing habit of humming while playing but she managed to use only her bidding box during this auction.

She opened 1♠. She denied shortness and showed a minimum in reply to North's 2NT Jacoby Forcing Raise. She showed two keys and the ♠Q in reply to his Roman Keycard Blackwood 4NT, but denied any outside kings with her 6♠ reply to his 5NT Specific King Ask. North settled for 6♠.

Mitzi won West's ♣10 opening lead with dummy's ♣K and hummed *The Four Rivers* while winning Tricks 2, 3 and 4 with the ♣A, ♠A and ♡A. Then she modulated to Brahms' Lullaby and led the ◊A. Finally she cashed the ♠K and two more hearts. When Mitzi led another diamond at Trick 9, Cora won the ◊K and was endplayed. She exited in clubs, Mitzi ruffed in dummy, threw her last diamond from her hand, and claimed the slam.

Whose fault?

Danny's fault. When Mitzi hummed Brahms' Lullaby, he had to hum *Wake Up, Wake Up, Darling' Corey!* Then Cora might awaken in time to see the strip-and-endplay coming and drop her diamond king under Mitzi's ace.

DEAL 138. WRONG SLAM

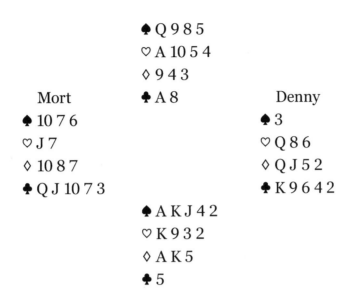

♠ Q 9 8 5
♡ A 10 5 4
◊ 9 4 3
♣ A 8

Mort

♠ 10 7 6
♡ J 7
◊ 10 8 7
♣ Q J 10 7 3

Denny

♠ 3
♡ Q 8 6
◊ Q J 5 2
♣ K 9 6 4 2

♠ A K J 4 2
♡ K 9 3 2
◊ A K 5
♣ 5

North had a classic limit raise of South's 1♠ opening and by a series of cue bids they reached 6♠.

West led the ♣Q. South won in dummy, ruffed a club and drew trump. Then he played the ◊A, ◊K and another diamond to East's ◊J.

Not wanting to offer a ruff-sluff, he switched to the ♡6. Declarer captured West's ♡J with dummy's ♡A and finessed the ♡9 on the way back. When it held, he made 6♡.

West, Post-Mortimer Snide, lectured his partner: "You needed to shift to the queen of hearts, not the six. Then declarer might have misguessed."

"Oh yeah?" countered East, Denny Decimal. "He surely wouldn't. Even a beginner knows to play for split honors. Besides, what if you had the *nine* of hearts instead of the *seven*?"

Who was right?

Denny was less wrong than Mort, but both missed the point. By the time Denny won the ◊J, South was marked with a 5=4=3=1 pattern, so a ruff-sluff could do declarer no good; he'd still have a heart loser. Upon winning the diamond, Denny's best and winning exit was in clubs.

Oh, anyone for playing in 6♡ instead of 6♠? That would work ... on this deal. But don't try to bid it. Too much can go wrong along the way.

DEAL 139. THIRD HAND PROBLEM

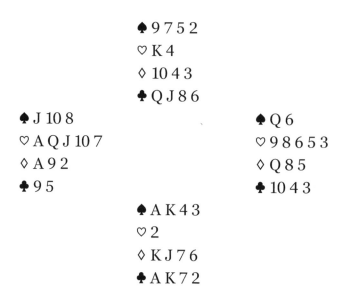

```
              ♠ 9 7 5 2
              ♡ K 4
              ◇ 10 4 3
              ♣ Q J 8 6
♠ J 10 8                        ♠ Q 6
♡ A Q J 10 7                    ♡ 9 8 6 5 3
◇ A 9 2                         ◇ Q 8 5
♣ 9 5                           ♣ 10 4 3
              ♠ A K 4 3
              ♡ 2
              ◇ K J 7 6
              ♣ A K 7 2
```

South opened 1♣, West overcalled 1♡, North raised to 2♣ and East raised to 2♡. When South bid 2♠ next, North felt compelled to show his four-card support and raise to 3♠. Not visualizing the duplication in hearts, South pushed on to 4♠.

West led the ♡A and continued the ♡10 to dummy's ♡K. South discarded the ◇7 and cashed both top spades. Then he took the ♣A, ♣K and ♣J. Not wanting to be endplayed, West discarded a heart. But the endplay was coming, as declarer threw West in with the master trump.

West coped by shifting to the ◇2. Declarer played low from dummy and captured East's ◇Q with the ◇K. Now a low diamond to dummy's ◇10 ensured the contract. South made 4♠ by the skin of this teeth.

Could the defenders have stopped him?

Yes. East had to preserve his ◇Q to avoid empowering dummy's ◇10. The ◇8 would have done the job. Diamonds were a frozen suit and East's ◇8 was the only card to keep them frozen.

DEAL 140. HARD TO SEE IT COMING

♠ 10 9 2
♡ J 7 6 3
◇ 5 3
♣ Q 9 5 2

♠ J 6
♡ K Q 8 5 4
◇ 10 7 2
♣ A K 8

♠ K Q 8 7 5
♡ 10 9
◇ 8 4
♣ 10 6 4 3

♠ A 4 3
♡ A 2
◇ A K Q J 9 6
♣ J 7

After East responded 1♠ to West's 1♡ opening, South's 3NT jump ended the auction.

West led the ♠J, which held, as East encouraged with the ♠8. West continued with the ♠6. Declarer captured East's ♠Q with the ♠A and ran diamonds. West discarded two low hearts and then the ♠8, East discarded all his clubs.

Meanwhile, declarer was discarding a club, a heart and a spade from dummy, and finally, after West discarded the ♠8, another club.

Declarer led the ♣J. West took both top clubs and shifted to the ♡K. South won the ♡A and led the ♡2 to West's ♡Q. Dummy's ♡J won Trick 13. That was declarer's ninth trick. 3NT made.

Could the defenders have kept declarer from winning a ninth trick?

Yes. West should have seen the endplay coming, though it wasn't easy. On the auction, West could count South for eight winners: six running diamonds and two major-suit aces. He had to hope South had no more than two hearts and two clubs.

Visualizing the cards this way, West must cash the ♣K and ♣A before leading his last spade. Then he can't be thrown in later with a club and forced to break hearts.

DEAL 141. EARLY TO RISE

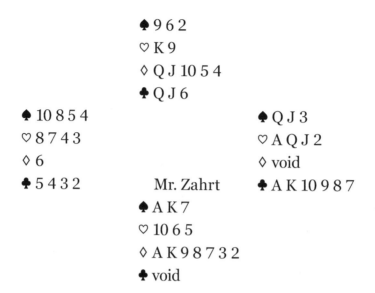

```
                    ♠ 9 6 2
                    ♡ K 9
                    ◊ Q J 10 5 4
                    ♣ Q J 6
    ♠ 10 8 5 4                         ♠ Q J 3
    ♡ 8 7 4 3                          ♡ A Q J 2
    ◊ 6                                ◊ void
    ♣ 5 4 3 2         Mr. Zahrt        ♣ A K 10 9 8 7
                    ♠ A K 7
                    ♡ 10 6 5
                    ◊ A K 9 8 7 3 2
                    ♣ void
```

East opened 1♣ in second seat. Playing old-fashioned Strong Jump Overcalls, South, Mr. Zahrt, jumped to 2◊. His very modern partner cue-bid 3♣ to deny a yarborough. East made a "You can't make that!" double. South avoided complications by jumping to 5◊, which ended the auction.

West led the ♣2. On seeing dummy, South said, "Couldn't you just have bid three notrump?" and played dummy's ♣J, covered by East's ♣K.

South pulled the ♣A from his hand to capture the ♣K but saw just in time that it was actually the ♠A and retracted it.

"Penalty card!" said East.

"Oh really?" asked South. "They must have changed the rules since the days when I played regularly."

So he ruffed and then played the ♠A. He led low to dummy's ◊10 to ruff a second club, then low to dummy's ◊J to ruff dummy's last club. He cashed the ♠K and led his last spade to East's ♠Q. East was endplayed

and had to offer a ruff-sluff or break hearts. He cashed the ♡A. 5◊ made.

But was 5◊ beatable?

Yes. If East sees the endplay coming, he dumps the ♠J and ♠Q under South's ♠A and ♠K, relying on West to hold the ♠10. Not too much to ask!

DEAL 142. "THIRD HAND HIGH!"

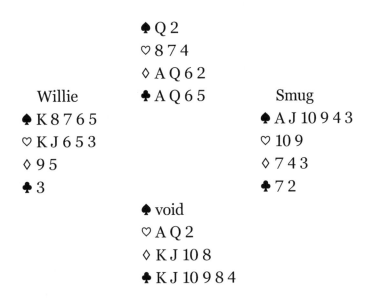

```
                    ♠ Q 2
                    ♡ 8 7 4
                    ◊ A Q 6 2
        Willie       ♣ A Q 6 5      Smug
     ♠ K 8 7 6 5                 ♠ A J 10 9 4 3
     ♡ K J 6 5 3                 ♡ 10 9
     ◊ 9 5                       ◊ 7 4 3
     ♣ 3                         ♣ 7 2
                    ♠ void
                    ♡ A Q 2
                    ◊ K J 10 8
                    ♣ K J 10 9 8 4
```

East, Mr. Smug, opened a Weak 2♠ Bid. South overcalled 3♣, hoping to double if West's expected spade raise came back to him. Not vul against vul, however West, Futile Willie, jumped to 5♠, deeming it a good sacrifice. North had been about to bid 5♣ but now she bid 6♣ and everyone passed.

West   led the ♠6. South played low from dummy and ruffed East's ♠A.

Declarer drew trump and cashed four diamonds ending in dummy. Then he led dummy's ♠Q and feigned astonishment when East followed low. As he discarded the ♡2, he turned to East and said, "Did you forget to play your king, old buddy? I think you did."

Mr. Smug grinned but did not answer.

Willie grinned too as he won the ♠K and exited with a low heart. But that was all for the defense. South won the ♡Q and had the rest. 6♣ made.

"I see you're up to your old tricks, Willie," said the scowling Mr. Smug.

"Save against five but forget to save again when you push them to six."

Willie hung his head in shame, but was he really to blame?

Maybe. And maybe Mame, North, was to blame for taking the push to 6♣. But East was surely to blame. West's ♠6 could only be from the ♠K and length. East must play the ♠9 and keep the ♠A to cover dummy's ♠Q later.

DEAL 143. WHAT'S THE HURRY?

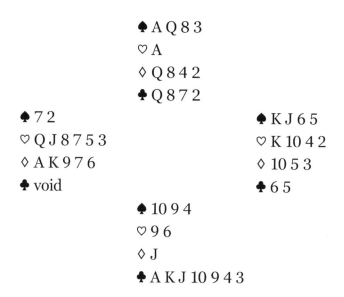

```
                    ♠ A Q 8 3
                    ♡ A
                    ◇ Q 8 4 2
                    ♣ Q 8 7 2
  ♠ 7 2                              ♠ K J 6 5
  ♡ Q J 8 7 5 3                      ♡ K 10 4 2
  ◇ A K 9 7 6                        ◇ 10 5 3
  ♣ void                             ♣ 6 5
                    ♠ 10 9 4
                    ♡ 9 6
                    ◇ J
                    ♣ A K J 10 9 4 3
```

South opened 3♣ with both sides vulnerable and West risked a 3♡ overcall. North bid the cold 3NT but East's 4♡ raise pushed him to 5♣. There the bidding ended, East being unwilling to suffer a sure doubled penalty sacrificing against a contract he thought he might beat.

West led the ◇A, showing the ◇K. East's ◇3 showed an odd number of diamonds, unlikely to be only one on the auction. West saw no reason to do anything special and exited safely with the ♡7.

Declarer won dummy's ♡A and ruffed a diamond, hoping the lead had been from ◇AKx. He cashed the ♣A and drew East's last trump with the ♣Q. Then ruffed another diamond, hoping the ◇K would fall. No such luck. Finally, he stripped the red suits by ruffing his last heart in dummy and then the ◇Q in hand.

Having set the stage, declarer led the ♠10 and let it ride. When East won the ♠J, he struck his forehead and said, "Don't tell me you have *both* missing spade honors! Why don't my finesses ever win?"

But it mattered not. East was endplayed. He exited with the ♡K. South shed a spade from his hand, ruffed in dummy, cashed dummy's ♠A. 5♣ made. "I knew I should have saved!" said West. Was he right?

No, he was wrong. He should have led the ♠7 to Trick 2, to protect East against the upcoming endplay and beat 5♣.

DEAL 144. LITTLE THINGS MEAN A LOT

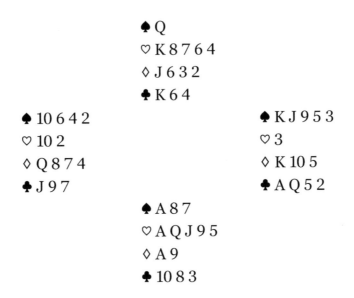

♠ Q
♡ K 8 7 6 4
♢ J 6 3 2
♣ K 6 4

♠ 10 6 4 2
♡ 10 2
♢ Q 8 7 4
♣ J 9 7

♠ K J 9 5 3
♡ 3
♢ K 10 5
♣ A Q 5 2

♠ A 8 7
♡ A Q J 9 5
♢ A 9
♣ 10 8 3

East opened 1♠, South overcalled 2♡ and North's 4♡ ended the auction. West led the ♠2 and declarer captured East's ♠K with the ♠A.

When he led the ♢A and let the ♢9 ride, it was beginning to look like an elimination deal.

East won the ♢10 and tried to cash the ♢K, but South ruffed high, ruffed a spade in dummy, ruffed dummy's last diamond and drew trump with his remaining two honors. Then he led his last spade, the ♠8. When West followed with the ♠8, declarer discarded the ♣4 from dummy. East had ♠J9 left and won the ♠9.

Rightly reluctant to lead from his club tenace, East led the ♠J. But declarer discarded a club from his hand and ruffed in dummy. Declarer lost two club tricks to East but made 4♡.

Could East have gotten off the endplay and beaten 4♡?

No. East couldn't, but *West* could have covered declarer's ♠8 with the ♠10 to *take East off the endplay* and beat 4♡.

DEAL 145. DECLARE OR DEFEND?

♠ K 7
♡ Q 5 2
◊ A 7 6 5
♣ 9 6 4 2

♠ A 8
♡ A J 6
◊ Q J 10 9 4 3 2
♣ J

With neither side vulnerable, East, Futile Willie, opens 3♡. You venture 4◊ and partner bids 5◊ over West's 5♣. West, the Unlucky Expert, leads the ♣K and East plays the ♣3.

Do you expect to make 5◊ or would you rather defend against it?

Make up your mind before reading further.

Did you opt to declare? West continues with the ♣10. East discards a heart and you ruff. You see two more possible losers, a heart and the ◊K. If you can avoid losing to the ◊K, you are home. It sure looks like you can, for East didn't ruff the second club, which suggests he has no diamonds.

Or maybe he has ◊K8 doubleton and didn't want to ruff with a natural trump trick; he would sure look foolish if you overruffed and then picked off his blanked ◊K. Or maybe he is being tricky with a singleton ◊K and is confident that he will win it on a finesse if he doesn't ruff now.

So will you take that finesse now?

If you do, you're going down. East was indeed being tricky. He wins a singleton ◊K, exits in spades, and waits for a heart trick. Down one. And now you must listen to him gloat, "Simon asked, 'Lunatic or genius?' Well now, everybody knows: I'm a *genius*!"

But you can make 5◊ by taking the ♠K followed by ♠A and *then* leading the ◊Q, letting it ride if West plays the ◊8, winning the ◊A if not. Losing to East's ◊K now won't hurt you, as he'll be endplayed. Did you opt to defend? Continue on to the next page.

Even after reading the above?

♠ K 7
♡ Q 5 2
◊ A 7 6 5
♣ 9 6 4 2

♠ J 10 4 2
♡ K 10 9 8 7 4 3
◊ K
♣ 3

Partner leads the ♣K and it wins. Then he continues with the ♣10. If you defend as Futile Willie did, declarer can make 5◊ as already shown. Even if she's Mrs. Guggenheim, for she read in the *Official Encyclopedia of Bridge* (under "Suit Combinations" that with only the king and a low card missing it's best to play for the drop),

So have you any hope?

Yes. Your partner saw you open 3♡, didn't he? But he didn't lead hearts. Not to Trick 1 and not to Trick 2. Do you wonder why?

Because he hasn't any. So ruff with your ◊K and return a heart for partner to ruff with his own singleton trump. Down one, the sure way